Comparable worth
and gender discrimination:

An international perspective

Morley Gunderson

International Labour Office   Geneva

Gunderson, M.
Comparable worth and gender discrimination: An international perspective
Geneva, International Labour Office, 1994
/Work of comparable worth/, /Equal pay/, /Wage differential/, /Men/, /Woman worker/, /Public sector/, /Private sector/, /OECD country/. 13.01.3
ISBN 92-2-108743-3

ILO Cataloguing in Publication Data

Printed in Switzerland   HEL

Comparable worth and gender discrimination:
An international perspective

PREFACE

This volume on *Comparable worth and gender discrimination: An international perspective*, by Morley Gunderson, Director of the Centre for Industrial Relations and Professor of the Department of Economics at the University of Toronto, is one of the outputs of the ILO Interdepartmental Project on Equality for Women in Employment. The document examines, inter alia, the definition of the concept of "comparable worth", and identifies the issues involved in its design, application and implementation. Furthermore, it assesses the application of the policy of comparable worth in Canada, the United States, as well as other developed and developing countries, in both the public and private sectors. Evidence on impact is also provided.

Internationally, the term comparable worth is taken to mean equal pay for work of equal value, or pay equity, involving various implementation steps within the enterprise. These consist of the identification of male- or female-dominated jobs, a gender-neutral job description, objective job evaluation, and an adjustment of pay in undervalued female-dominated jobs. Settlements tend to be reasonably large, in some cases as high as 30 per cent, but usually averaging around 20 per cent.

The volume perceives comparable worth policy as having a larger potential scope than some conventional equal pay policies for reducing the earnings gap between men and women. Comparable worth can deal with pay differences arising from occupational segregation (an important contributor to the male-female earnings gap), while conventional equal pay policy tends to be restricted to comparisons within the same job in the organization. Comparable worth requires that male-dominated and female-dominated jobs in the same enterprise receive equal pay for work of equal value and that this job value be determined by objective measures based on job evaluation, which take into consideration the required skill, effort, responsibility and working conditions in the job.

Despite its advantages, the book shows that the effectiveness of the policy is limited by a number of factors. For example, comparisons tend to

V

be generally restricted to jobs within the same organization and, therefore, it cannot deal with the earnings gap arising from the fact that women are disproportionately employed in low-wage establishments and industries. Furthermore, within establishments its scope is restricted to situations where comparable value can be established. Moreover, it does not deal with the portion of the pay gap arising from such differences as education, training and work experience. In view of the above, the volume points out that while comparable worth is an important policy, equal employment opportunity policies and legislation that prohibit discrimination in recruitment and promotion and also attempt to facilitate the employment participation of women and men on a more equal basis (such as through education and training programmes, child care and parental measures) are more likely to have a greater potential than comparable worth policy in reducing significantly the gender pay gap.

This volume was prepared as part of a work item on measuring wage differentials under the responsibility of Richard Anker within the International Labour Office's Interdepartmental Project on Equality for Women in Employment under implementation in the 1992-93 biennium. The project has tried to promote, in a multidisciplinary way, the examination of some of the critical issues concerning gender equality in the employment field with a view to achieving a more comprehensive understanding of the linkages between the different elements at play in this area. The data generated and the insight gained by the project could serve as a strong basis for planning future and more effective action to advance the course of gender equality. The project hopes that this particular volume by Professor Gunderson could provide guidance to the various relevant groups in the attempt to strengthen action to promote gender equity in pay.

Eugenia Date-Bah,
Manager,
Interdepartmental Project on
Equality for Women in Employment,
International Labour Office,
Geneva, Switzerland.

CONTENTS

INTRODUCTION

1

On an international basis, the changing labour market behaviour of women has had profound implications for a wide range of issues, many of which themselves are of current policy concern. These include issues as diverse as: fertility and family formation; wage inequality; poverty and income distribution; the demand for child care; pressures for increased flexibility of working time; the role of collective bargaining and the demand for unionization; and the changing nature of household tasks and responsibilities.

This changing role of women and the increased awareness of the inequality of their position with respect to men has brought international and national attention to women's issues. This is manifest, for example, in the fact that 1975 was declared International Women's Year, and the decade 1976-1985 was declared the United Nations Decade for Women. Numerous national policies and measures have also been adopted to deal with gender discrimination, and to facilitate the labour market adaptability of women. These changes have brought greater awareness and policy attention to the fact that unequal pay between men and women also tends to be a universal phenomenon.

The empirical evidence, presented later, indicates that even when one controls for a wide range of productivity-related characteristics that determine wages, a sizeable male-female wage gap still prevails. Much of that gap reflects the fact that women tend to work in female-dominated occupations that are low paid. Even when these occupations involve the same skill, effort, responsibility and working conditions as the male-dominated jobs, they tend to pay less than the male-dominated jobs. This has given rise to the rationale for policies of equal pay for work of equal value – the focus of this volume.

While the empirical evidence does suggest that a portion of the wage gap does reflect wage discrimination – including unequal pay for work of equal value – it is important to emphasize that policy responses may be appropriate even if the pay gap did not reflect discrimination. Unequal

1

outcomes in the labour market may be socially unacceptable even if they are generated by processes other than discrimination.⌐

1.1 SOME TERMINOLOGY

The terms "equal pay for work of equal value", "comparable worth" and "pay equity" are usually used interchangeably, although at times distinctions are made. Comparable worth is usually the term used in the United States (where the policy was first instituted in some state governments), although sometimes it is used to distinguish between situations when the value of the jobs only have to be comparable or substantially similar as opposed to identical or precisely equal before comparisons can be made. Pay equity is the term usually used in Canada (where the policy seems to be most extensively applied), although at times it is used to imply the goal of moving towards pay equality between men and women, with comparable worth being simply one of many mechanisms for achieving that goal. The term equal pay for work of equal value is usually used internationally, although comparable worth and pay equity have increasingly been used.

Throughout this volume, the terms will be used interchangeably, although the shorter phrase comparable worth will be used most often because it seems to have been identified most clearly with the concept. The concept of comparable worth is taken here to be one where equal pay is required between male-dominated and female-dominated jobs that are of comparable worth or value, where such value is determined by objective measures (such as job evaluation) involving comparisons of the skill, effort, responsibility, and working conditions required in the jobs. Usually the concept applies to comparisons within the same organization or establishment (i.e. for the same employer) although the necessity of this requirement is subject to legitimate debate.

As discussed later, there are numerous contentious issues surrounding this concept or working definition. These include the definition of gender dominance and whether the jobs have to be gender dominated before comparisons can be made, whether the values of the job have to be equal or only comparable in some way, whether the values have to be measured by job evaluation procedures, and whether comparisons can only be made within the same establishment.

One further point of terminology: the literature on discrimination often makes a distinction between sex and gender, with sex referring to the biological difference, and gender referring to the social and cultural constructs. Even though the common term sex discrimination is often used here (as is the case in most legislation), recognition should be given to the fact that such discrimination is socially and culturally determined.

1.2   INTERNATIONAL PERSPECTIVE

The emphasis in this book is on comparable worth in an international context. It is beyond the scope of the volume, however, to provide a comprehensive picture of discrimination and the policy responses in different countries. Information from specific countries will be employed on an illustrative rather than comprehensive basis. The emphasis is on how comparable worth may or may not work in different labour market systems, with specific countries being used mainly to illustrate those systems.

This international focus is important not only because it provides comparisons based on experience in different situations, but also because it facilitates emulating the successes and avoiding the mistakes of others. The international comparisons are also important because greater international trade and capital mobility requires greater coordination of policy responses to social problems. Countries may find it difficult to compete with other countries that do not have similar labour standards, including ones pertaining to discrimination. Greater integration of world economies may require greater integration and harmonization of policy responses to deal with social problems. The sensible integration of policy responses, however, requires information on how the policies have been applied and how they have functioned in different countries where they have been applied. The purpose of this volume is to provide such information for one such policy – comparable worth.

1.3   FORMAT OF VOLUME

Chapter 1 provides an introduction to the subject with definitions of the main concepts. Chapter 2 deals with the potential sources of the inequality in pay between men and women as well as the empirical evidence on the relative importance of these different sources of pay inequality, with particular emphasis on the implication for different policy responses (Chapter 3). Chapter 4 analyses the concept of comparable worth; the steps involved in its application (Chapter 5); additional design and implementation issues (Chapter 6); and its legislative application in different countries (Chapter 7). The impact of theoretically expected comparable worth is examined in Chapter 8; evidence on its impact in cases where it has been applied is dealt with in Chapter 9; and more aggregate information on its impact on the wage gap, employment and other aspects of behaviour appears in Chapter 10. The last three chapters provide an analysis of the feasibility and pros and cons of applying comparable worth to specific situations: the private sector (Chapter 11); and countries with different legal and labour market systems (Chapter 12). Chapter 13 provides a summary and suggestions for further research and analysis.

POSSIBLE SOURCES OF INEQUALITY IN PAY

2

Since the appropriate policy response depends upon the source of the pay inequality between men and women, it is important to have a reasonable understanding of the sources of inequality, and especially those sources that are amenable to redress through comparable worth policies. In this chapter, the possible sources of pay inequality between men and women are discussed. The first section deals with the theoretically expected determinants of the pay gap. The second section deals briefly with the methodologies that have been used to estimate the actual determinants of the gap, and the third section provides empirical evidence on those determinants.

2.1 THEORETICALLY EXPECTED DETERMINANTS

The average pay gap between men and women is obviously a result of the pay received by individual men and women and hence it reflects all determinants of individual compensation. As such, it reflects a person's occupation, industry, region and the type of enterprise in which they work. For purposes of determining the appropriate policy response, it is useful to categorize the possible sources of inequality of pay between men and women into the following categories: differences in human capital endowments; differences in jobs desired; differences in jobs available; differences in pay for the same work; and differences in pay for work of "equal value". Each of these sources will be examined in turn.

Differences in human capital

Wages reflect an economic return to human capital, whether that human capital is acquired (e.g. education, training, experience) or endowed (e.g. dexterity, strength, intelligence). With respect to endowed characteristics, there is little reason to expect substantial systematic differences between men and women, or where they may exist (e.g. physical strength) it seems reasonable to assume that they tend to be offset by other factors such as dexterity, or that they do not matter for most modern jobs. This is the case especially for individual workers in the light of the large overlap in such skills between men and women.

Some "endowed" characteristics may be culturally determined or at least heavily influenced by cultural and social norms. For example, women may be more caring and cooperative and influenced by subjective criteria, and men more self-interested and competitive and influenced by objective criteria. The latter characteristics may be more valued in the labour market, while the former are more valued within the family or within personal relationships. In fact, the former may tie women to the household and inhibit labour market activity, or crowd women into jobs that value these characteristics (e.g. nursing, elementary teaching). Whether these characteristics are "innate" or acquired through socialization and the family is not crucial from the perspective of labour market behaviour. What matters is that they can give rise to behaviour that is valued differently in the labour market than in other areas of interaction.

Acquired human capital is usually obtained as an investment whereby costs are incurred (often in the form of forgone earnings) in return for higher wages at some future time. Examples include education, training, labour mobility and job search. These are generally considered as "legitimate" sources of earnings inequality since they reflect an economic return for an investment.

Even in this area, however, the distinction between discrimination and choice can become blurred. Women may be compelled or encouraged to curtail their education, and they may be streamed by their family or by education institutions or even by peer pressure into certain types of education that is less labour-market-oriented – the humanities as opposed to the sciences, languages as opposed to maths. Employers may do the same with respect to training, and they may be reluctant to provide costly training if they perceive that it may be lost due to turnover or career interruptions.

Women may not invest in labour-market-oriented education or training if they feel that the returns will be artificially reduced by subsequent discrimination in the labour market. Considerable training, job search and labour-market information is acquired informally through such processes as networking on the job and the establishment of mentors. Many of these channels may be less available to women than to men. Different family responsibilities may also affect human capital investments. Being tied to the household may reduce the length of time spent in the labour market, and it may inhibit job and geographic mobility decisions, including decisions on commuting.

Differences in jobs desired

These same factors that affect human-capital investment decisions may also more directly affect the male-female wage differential by influencing the types of jobs that women choose. Women may choose jobs where it is easier to combine household work and child-care responsibilities with their paid employment. They may select occupations where there is relatively little loss of skills and depreciation of human capital from discontinuity or interruptions in their labour-market work. Women may choose jobs with flexible work schedules or with responsibilities, such as travel, that minimize conflict with household work. These are often choices that men do not have to make, at least to the extent that they do not have the same household responsibilities, especially associated with the bearing and raising of children. This is true in developing as well as developed countries (Palmer, 1991, p. 12).

Differences in jobs available

Employers may engage in gender stereotyping, restricting women from entering certain jobs and segregating them into others. The occupational segregation of women may affect their wages directly by segregating them into lower-wage jobs, and indirectly since "crowding" reduces wages in such jobs because there is an increased supply of labour competing for a restricted number of job openings. Occupational segregation on the part of employers may reflect their own preferences or perhaps erroneous perceptions based on stereotypes. They may also reflect the response of employers to the pressures of customers or co-workers. Co-workers especially may be reluctant to be supervised by women.

Unions can be an important vehicle for influencing the jobs available for women, and the remuneration for those jobs. The more overt forms of such discrimination, such as different collective agreement rates for men and women or the exclusion of women from certain craft jobs, are now a thing of the past. However, more indirect forms are possible. For example, unions can simply bargain harder for wage increases in male-dominated jobs. General union wage premiums may disproportionately go to males simply because males are more likely to be unionized. Unions may devote more organizing resources to the area of male-dominated jobs, or political resources to protect such jobs, for example, from plant closures or mass layoffs due to import competition. Unions can also bargain extensively for provisions such as seniority and restrictions on part-time workers or on subcontracting – provisions that may disproportionately help male members, perhaps even at the expense of female workers.

Of course, unions can also be a powerful force to facilitate greater equality of pay between men and women. In general, unions tend to reduce wage inequality, in part by bargaining for equal absolute wage increases which tend to reduce the skill differential. As discussed later, they

7

can be an important vehicle for the enforcement and administration of anti-discrimination legislation, especially regarding comparable worth. In countries with more centralized bargaining, male-female wage differentials can be reduced as part of a broader social policy – just as they could have been fostered if "male wages" were perceived as necessary for a "family wage" for the breadwinner, and females were perceived to work only for "pin money". In essence, being political institutions responding to the pressure of the rank-and-file in their constituency, unions can be a force that could either exacerbate or reduce male-female wage differentials and occupational segregation.

Differences in pay within the same occupation

The previous discussion referred to inequalities in pay between men and women that may arise because of differences in the occupations or types of job done by men and women. Such differences may reflect human capital endowments, as well as differences in the occupations "chosen" by women or made available to them by employers.

Differences in pay may also arise within the same occupation or job, and within the same establishment. Such pure wage discrimination is subject to conventional legislation on equal pay for equal work. In most circumstances, the work does not have to be identical in each and every respect. It only has to be substantially similar, with occasional differences (e.g. heavy lifting done by men) being allowed, especially if offset by other tasks done by women.

Such differences in pay for the same work (i.e. within the same narrowly defined job class) within the same firm is generally perceived to be quite small. This is so because it is the most overt form of wage discrimination and is subject to redress through conventional legislation requiring equal pay for equal work. Forces of competition, if they are allowed to operate, should also reduce such pure wage discrimination since firms have an economic incentive to utilize more of the lower wage labour to do the same tasks as the higher wage labour, if the wage differences reflect discrimination and not productivity differences. This should increase the demand for the lower wage labour relative to the higher wage group, until wages are equalized for the two groups.

While differences in pay for the same job are generally expected to be quite small *within* the same firm, this is not the case across firms, especially firms of different size. There is a well-established pattern for larger firms to pay higher wages, even after controlling for the effect of other factors such as unionization and market power that can affect wages. Also, some firms may pay "efficiency wage premiums" to reduce costly turnover or shirking or to induce loyalty and commitment to the firm since workers will be reluctant to lose such "good jobs". To the extent that there is a queue of applicants for these higher wage jobs, firms may ration these scarce jobs in part on the basis of discriminatory preferences. In essence, women may be disproportionately excluded from these high wage firms and jobs.

Wage differences for the same work may also prevail if they reflect compensating wages for other cost differences. Such cost differences could include costs arising from absenteeism or turnover, perhaps reflecting differences in household responsibilities between men and women. Such cost differences, however, are unlikely to be substantial within the same occupation because, if they were substantial, they would be more likely to lead to people being reallocated to different jobs rather than paid a different wage within the same job. In other areas, such as pension costs, there is controversy over whether they are greater for males or females.[1]

Differences in pay for work of equal value

For purposes of evaluating comparable worth initiatives, what matters are pay differences that exist across different occupations that are deemed to be of equal value. As indicated in more detail in the next two chapters, the different occupations are usually ones that are male-dominated compared to ones that are female-dominated. Value is usually determined by some administrative "objective" procedure such as job evaluation, and not on the basis of economic forces of supply and demand. Comparisons are usually made with occupations of *equal* value, although projections of expected value may be allowed. Under most current legal applications, comparisons are limited to within the same firm, although extended concepts could allow comparisons across different firms.

The key advance of comparable worth comparisons is that they allow comparisons across different occupations, as long as they are deemed of equal value according to some principle such as job evaluation. This is in contrast to conventional legislation on equal pay for equal work, where the comparisons are restricted to pay differences within the same job as well as within the same establishment.

2.2 METHODOLOGIES FOR MEASURING MALE-FEMALE PAY DIFFERENCES

Before providing some evidence on the relative importance of the different sources of pay inequality, it is informative to highlight briefly the different methodologies that have been used to estimate the determinants of the inequality.

Unadjusted earnings ratios

The simplest measure of pay inequality between men and women is the raw or unadjusted ratio of the average earnings of females relative to males. This is sometimes calculated separately for different subgroups of interest, such as full-time, full-year workers, or married workers or union versus non-union workers.

Because of its simplicity, this measure is readily understood and provides a convenient summary statistic of pay inequality. It highlights how that inequality differs by particular groups, and it can provide a useful picture of trends in time patterns if the composition of the workforce does not change dramatically. It does not, however, simultaneously control for the myriad of factors that influence the wage gap and therefore does not indicate the independent contribution to the earnings gap of each of those determinants.

Earnings ratios in narrowly defined occupations

Earnings ratios can be calculated in narrowly defined occupations that can be taken as approximating the same job. This could be the case, for example, with respect to occupational classifications at the three- or four-digit level, especially if subcategories are also used (e.g. light assembler, helper). The use of extremely narrowly defined occupations is useful because it controls for not only conventionally observable variables that can influence wages (e.g. education, training) but also conventionally unobservable factors (e.g. motivation, perseverance). It can reasonably be assumed that these factors trade off against each other so that persons who can do the particular job have the appropriate *bundle* of observable or unobservable characteristics, even though they may not be the same in each and every characteristic.

Regression procedures

The most common procedure for estimating the extent of discrimination and its determinants is to use a decomposition of the earnings gap based on regression analysis. The regression analysis facilitates controlling for the effect of the wide range of human capital and other determinants of earnings.

Typically, earnings equations are estimated separately for males and females, based on micro data with the individual worker as the unit of observation. The dependent variable in each of the male and female earnings equation is typically a measure of earnings or wages. The independent variables or determinants of earnings include the "endowments" of worker characteristics or human capital such as education, experience and training, as well as control variables such as race, marital status and location. The resulting estimated regression coefficients indicate the returns that the market "pays" for changes in such endowments as education and experience.

The average male-female wage differential is then decomposed into two component parts: one is attributed to differences in the endowments of wage-determining characteristics (mean values of the explanatory variables); the other component is attributed to differences in the economic returns to the same characteristics (differences in the regression coefficients). The estimating equations and the decomposition procedure, along with references to a number of empirical studies that have used the procedure, are contained in Gunderson (1989a).

Equal value wage lines

A recently applied procedure for estimating the extent of pay discrimination (more specifically, unequal pay for work of equal value) involves estimating equal value wage lines or pay lines (discussed in more detail in Chapter 5). Such pay lines essentially show the relationship between pay in particular jobs and the job evaluation points of those jobs. Separate pay lines are estimated for male-dominated jobs and for female-dominated jobs, with gender dominance usually being defined as involving a proportion of about 70 per cent or more of that particular sex. Differences in the height of the two pay lines indicate pay differences between jobs of equal value as indicated by equal job evaluation scores.

Regressions with percentage female in occupation as an explanatory variable

The equal value pay lines described above have generally been applied with respect to jobs with the same employer, usually a particular level of government. A related procedure for estimating wage differentials across occupations of the same value (and hence the potential impact of comparable worth) involves including the percentage female (i.e. feminization rate) in the individual's occupation as a regressor in the separate earnings equations for males and females based on micro data with the individual worker as the unit of observation. The rationale is that if the percentage female has a negative effect on earnings, after controlling for the effect of other variables that affect earnings, then unequal pay for work of equal value prevails. In this case value is not measured by job evaluation points but rather by the effect of human capital and other wage determinants included in the regression. Alternatively stated, if equal pay for work of equal value prevailed, then one would not expect any systematic relationship between pay and the feminization rate of the occupation. This would be true throughout the whole range of feminization rates in the occupation, or it could be confined to only female- and male-dominated jobs, if the equal value comparisons were limited only to gender-dominated jobs.

2.3   EVIDENCE ON DETERMINANTS OF INEQUALITY IN PAY

Reflecting the parts of the world where most of the empirical studies[2] have been conducted, the evidence is based largely on American and Canadian data. This qualification should be kept in mind when making generalizations about other economies, especially those of less developed countries.

The empirical studies indicate that even after controlling for a wide range of variables that influence wages, a male-female pay gap remains that most studies attribute to discrimination. Whether all of the unexplained gap can be attributed to discrimination, as opposed to other factors not controlled for in the analysis, is a matter of some debate in the literature. The gap may be reduced considerably by controlling for the effect of factors other than gender that affect wages, but it is seldom eliminated. When it is almost eliminated, that usually occurs by controlling for variables, whose differences themselves may reflect discrimination.

Factors arising from outside the labour market (e.g. within the household and educational institutions) appear to be a more important source of pay inequality than factors that originate from within the labour market. The gap is largest, for example, between married men and married women, with marriage having a large positive effect on the earnings of men, but a large negative effect on the earnings of women, likely reflecting differences in household responsibilities. This highlights the limited scope for labour market policies that deal with labour market discrimination, and the potentially broader scope for policies affecting such factors as child care and family planning.

Pay inequality arising from differences in the occupational distribution between men and women is likely to be a more important source of the earnings gap than are pay differences between men and women within the same narrowly defined occupation, especially within the same establishment. This highlights the potential scope of equal employment opportunity policies as well as non-labour market policies to improve the occupational distribution of women, in addition to comparable worth policies that allow comparisons across different occupations. It also highlights the limited scope of conventional equal pay policies that allow comparisons only within the same occupation and establishment.

Differences in pay across establishments are an important source of inequality of pay since women tend to be disproportionately employed in smaller, low-wage establishments. This limits the scope of equal pay policies in general (whether conventional equal pay for equal work or the broader comparable worth), which generally allow comparisons only within the same establishment. It highlights the greater potential for equal employment opportunity policies to open up jobs in high-wage establishments to women.

The productivity adjusted earnings gap tends to be greater in the private sector than in the public sector. This highlights the fact that comparable worth could have a greater potential impact in the private sector than in the public sector, given that the wage gap is greater in the private sector. Within the private sector itself, the productivity adjusted earnings gap tends to be smaller the greater the degree of competition in product markets, highlighting the fact that competitive forces can serve to reduce the extent of discrimination.

The earnings gap tends to be declining slowly over time. This is true in a wide range of industrialized countries. The extent to which this reflects changes in the composition of the male and female workforces, the impact of policy or other initiatives, or a decline in discrimination, has not been determined.[3]

The earnings gap tends to be smaller in countries[4] with centralized collective bargaining that emphasize egalitarian wage policies in general (e.g. Sweden, Norway and Australia). It tends to be largest in countries that emphasize a traditional, non-egalitarian role for women in the labour market (e.g. Japan) or that have decentralized, market-oriented wage determination with enterprise-level bargaining (e.g. United States and Canada). These latter countries also have a greater degree of wage inequality in general and this accounts for much of the greater earnings gap between men and women because women tend to be at the low end of the wage distribution (Blau and Kahn, 1992).

These generalizations suggest that institutional mechanisms such as centralized collective bargaining and wage tribunals can be a viable mechanism for reducing the earnings gap, especially if they involve egalitarian wage policies in general. Policies that increase low wages in general will also disproportionately increase women's wages and hence reduce the earnings gap.

Notes

[1] Moore (1987), for example, has argued that employers' pension costs are higher for females than males because women tend to live longer than men and therefore receive the pension for a longer period of time. In such circumstances, lower female wages may be necessary to offset the higher pension benefit they receive. Pesando, Gunderson and McLaren (1991), however, provide empirical evidence to indicate that this effect is more than offset by other factors that lead to lower pension benefits for women. Most importantly, women tend not to accumulate the seniority and seniority-based wage increases that accrue to men, and hence are less likely to receive early retirement subsidies that are based on years of service, and substantial pension benefit accruals that are based on final-years earnings. Also, in earnings based plans, lower wages due to discrimination become compounded into lower pension benefits. In such circumstances pensions exacerbate rather than offset the male-female wage differential. These studies focus on pension costs; they do not deal with differences in other related costs such as health costs.

[2] Reviews include Blau and Ferber (1987), Cain (1986). Gunderson (1989a), Lloyd and Neimi (1979), Madden (1985), Treiman and Hartman (1981), and Willborn (1986a).

[3] American studies (Blau and Beller, 1988; Blau and Ferber, 1987; O'Neill, 1985; and Smith and Ward, 1984) indicate that the overall gap has been fairly constant over the 1970s and 1980s. However, it would have widened over that period because of the compositional changes associated with the influx of younger women and women with little labour market experience. After control-

ling for these compositional changes, the gap did narrow somewhat. In Canada, Shapiro and Stelcner (1987) indicate that about half of the decline in the gap over the 1980s can be attributed to improvements in the productivity-related characteristics of women relative to men, and half to a reduction in discrimination.

[4] International comparisons of the earnings gap are given in Blau and Kahn (1992), Ferber (1991), Gregory and Daly (1991), Gunderson (1989a), Mincer (1985), Organization for Economic Cooperation and Development (1991a, 1991b), and Treiman and Roos (1983).

SCOPE AND ACTUAL IMPACT
OF DIFFERENT POLICY INITIATIVES

3

The previously discussed determinants of pay inequality between men and women have implications for the potential scope of various policy initiatives since the different policies can affect different aspects of the wage gap. In this chapter, the different initiatives will be briefly discussed with particular emphasis on their potential scope to reduce the earnings gap, given the different determinants of the gap.

3.1 POLICY INITIATIVES AND POTENTIAL SCOPE TO REDUCE PAY INEQUALITY

Equal pay policies, including comparable worth

Equal pay policies have the common characteristic that they affect the pay of women. Conventional equal pay policies that require equal pay for equal work are likely to have only a small impact since their scope is severely limited by the fact that the wage gap is generally very small (e.g. in the region of 5 per cent in the United States and Canada) between men and women in the same occupation and the same establishment. Furthermore, the implementation of such policies can be limited by the fact that they have to be initiated by a complaint, the complaint is difficult to prove, and complaints may be costly and subject to retribution. Comparable worth policies have greater potential scope since they allow comparisons across different occupations as long as the jobs are of equal value, and pay differences arising from differences in the occupational distribution of men and women are generally perceived to be a more important contributor to the pay gap than are pay differences arising from within the same occupation.

Equal employment opportunity legislation, including affirmative action

Equal employment opportunity legislation has the common characteristic that it increases the demand for female labour. Conventional equal employment opportunity legislation does so by prohibiting discrimination in the various phases of the employment decision; recruiting, hiring, training, promotion and dismissals.

Affirmative action is a stronger form of intervention in this respect, requiring positive actions to overcome the legacy of the past history of discrimination and to compensate for unequal starting points. Usually, four steps are involved:

(i)   an internal audit within the firm to establish the number and position of the groups subject to affirmative action;

(ii) a comparison of these numbers with the representation of these groups in the externally available labour market;

(iii) the establishment of goals or targets (perhaps even quantitabive quotas) to ensure that the internal representation of these groups is representative of their availability in the relevant external labour market; and

(iv) the establishment of a plan and timetable for achieving these targets.

While equal employment opportunity and affirmative action legislation is generally designed to increase employment opportunities and to reduce occupational segregation, this can have an indirect effect on the wages of women by increasing the demand for women and enabling them to move into higher wage occupations. In fact, economists tend to have a preference for equal employment opportunity policies over wage-fixing policies such as equal pay, because the former can increase *both* wages and employment (by increasing the demand for women) while wage-fixing policies may reduce the demand for women because of the higher wages.

The potential for equal employment opportunity policies to reduce pay inequality between men and women is quite substantial because they can deal with almost all components of the pay gap. They can deal with the (likely) small component that can be attributed to pay differences between men and women in the same occupation within the same establishment, because the demand for women will be increased relative to the demand for men and this should serve to raise their wages within all occupational groups. Equal employment opportunity policies can deal with the (likely) larger portion of the gap that is attributable to differences in the occupational distribution between men and women in that they should disproportionately serve to increase the demand for women at higher occupational positions because these are the positions from which women otherwise tend to be excluded. Equal employment opportunity programmes may also reduce the wage discrimination that can prevail across firms since those that discriminate most will be under most pressure to meet their targets. Equal employment opportunity legislation may even deal with wage inequality that simply reflects inequalities in opportunity even if they do not arise from discrimination within the labour market.

Facilitating policies

Facilitating policies are those that encourage the labour market participation of women to place them on a more equal footing with that of men. They reduce the barriers that otherwise inhibit the equal participation of women. Outside the labour market, such policies include those pertaining to the educational streaming of girls, as well as the availability of child care and elder care (since the care of both children and elder family members disproportionately falls on women). In some countries, housing availability and commuting problems are important barriers. Within the family, such policies can include those relating to divorce (to reduce the restrictive ties that many women have with respect to their husbands) as well as family planning (given the importance of child-rearing activities on the labour-market behaviour of women). Within the labour market itself, such facilitating policies include those concerning parental leave, flexible working time and training programmes, as well as the unionization of women.

The potential for facilitating policies to reduce pay inequality between men and women is likely to be quite substantial given the fact that pay inequality arising from factors outside the labour market is likely to be a more important contributor to the wage gap than are factors arising from within the labour market itself. Furthermore, the facilitating policies can deal with pay inequality that may not reflect discrimination in the labour market, but rather may simply be a result of the legacy of social and family practices that disproportionately burden women relative to men in the labour market. By dealing with ingrained attitudes and prejudices, including those of women themselves, such policies may also have a more lasting effect, without engendering the backlashes that are common with anti-discrimination policies.

3.2   ACTUAL IMPACT OF DIFFERENT POLICY INITIATIVES

The previous discussion focused on the potential scope of the different policy initiatives to reduce pay inequality between men and women, given the determinants or sources of that pay inequality. In this section, evidence on the actual impact of different policy issues is discussed. (Specific legislative details of the policy are discussed in Chapter 7.) This is informative in its own right, but it also serves to put comparable worth in the broader picture of these alternative and co-existing policies. Furthermore, it is useful information from which to make inferences about the possible sources of inequality in pay. For example, policies may have been ineffective in reducing the pay gap in part because they only dealt with a small portion of the gap.

The impact of conventional policies of equal pay for equal work have been analysed for the province of Ontario in Canada. Econometric analysis based on both cross-sectional data (Gunderson, 1975) and time series data (Gunderson, 1985) indicate the policy to have had no significant effect on narrowing the male-female wage gap. Plausible reasons offered for this unexpected result were the limited scope for such a policy given that it can only deal with wage differences within the same occupation and establishment, and that it required a complaint to be made before an investigation was initiated.

In contrast, equal pay policies in Britain seemed to have had a more substantial impact on reducing the male-female wage gap. Zabalza and Tzannatos (1985a, 1985b) indicate that the ratio of female to male hourly earnings increased from 0.58 in 1970 to 0.66 in 1975, which was the period over which the Equal Pay Act was put in place (passed in 1970 to be implemented by 1975). This increase of 0.08 in the wage ratio implies a reduction of almost 20 per cent of the wage gap of 0.42. They indicate that compositional changes in the workforce did not account for any of the increase in the wage ratio. The increase occurred largely through changes in job rates in collective agreements which covered about 60 per cent of the workforce and which eliminated differences in the minimum job rates between male and female jobs. This positive effect of equal pay legislation in Britain as compared to Canada suggests that the legislation is likely to be more effective when it is incorporated into the more formalized process of collective bargaining, rather than relying on complaints to ensure compliance.

Chiplin et al. (1980) also find the British equal pay legislation to be associated with a 0.08 increase in the ratio of female-to-male hourly earnings, after econometrically controlling for the effect of the business cycle and trend in the ratio. They argue that much of this may be attributed to the incomes policy that was introduced in 1973 and which reduced the male-female wage gap by allowing a flat rate increase which would imply a larger relative increase for low-wage females as opposed to higher-wage males. To the extent that the flat rate increases were allowed so as to accommodate equal pay adjustments, this still suggests that the equal pay legislation had a positive impact. It does, however, indicate the difficulty of separating out the independent impact of different laws that can all affect the earnings gap. This is also likely to be even more true of the equal employment opportunity legislation embodied in the Sex Discrimination Act of 1975, and which may have raised female wages by increasing the demand for females relative to males.

In the United States, both equal pay and equal employment opportunity initiatives are combined in the same legislation (Title VII or the Equal Employment Opportunity provision of the Civil Rights Act of 1964). Econometric evaluation of that legislation (reviewed in Gunderson, 1989a) generally finds it to have increased the ratio of female to male earnings or to have reduced occupational segregation which should indirectly reduce pay inequality. However, some studies find no impact on earnings, and the quantitative magnitude of the impact, when it was reported, was generally small.

Affirmative action initiatives in the United States (under the Federal Contract Compliance Program of Executive Order 11246) do seem to have had more positive effects, but only when they were directed at women (econometric studies in this area are reviewed in Gunderson, 1989a). In fact, in the earlier period of the legislation when it was directed mainly at Blacks, it improved their position but had a negative effect on the earnings and employment opportunities of women. However, in the mid 1970s, when affirmative action was redirected more towards women, it benefited women in a number of dimensions (occupational advance, reductions in quit rates, and increases in employment growth) that should also reduce pay inequality (the latter not being directly measured in those studies).

Australian equal pay initiatives have been called comparable worth initiatives and yet they are not comparable worth initiatives in the conventional sense based on objective measures of the worth of a job through job evaluation procedures. Rather, they involve wage awards that were larger for females than for males in their unique system of wage arbitration awards. In that decree system, regional and federal tribunals make wage awards for the vast majority of the workforce in the private as well as the public sector. Female wages were originally officially set at 54 per cent of male wages for the same job, and this was raised to 75 per cent in 1949. In 1969, a policy of equal pay for equal work was adopted in that the official markdown for women in the same job was eliminated. While equal pay was required within the same job, female-dominated jobs were still awarded lower wages. In 1972, the official markdown of female-dominated jobs relative to male-dominated jobs was also eliminated. This has been termed a policy of equal pay for equal value or comparable worth in that it was to eliminate the official mark-down that prevailed for female-dominated jobs.

Gregory and Duncan (1981, 1983) indicate that the ratio of female to male award wages increased from 0.72 in 1969 at the time of the equal pay awards (eliminating wage differences within the same job), to 0.77 in 1972 at the time of the equal value awards (eliminating official wage differences between male-dominated and female-dominated jobs) and to 0.93 by 1977. These results suggest that official state policies can be used to institutionalize discrimination, but that these same policies can also be reversed to be an effective mechanism to reduce pay inequality. In addition, reductions in pay inequality are facilitated by centralized, formal systems of wage determination, as opposed to more decentralized market-based systems.

3.3 IMPLICATIONS FOR SCOPE OF INITIATIVES AND FOR SOURCES OF PAY GAP

While the international evidence on the impact of policy initiatives is not comprehensive, it suggests some generalizations about the potential scope of the policy initiatives and about the possible sources of inequality in pay.

The scope of conventional equal pay initiatives is likely to be severely restricted when comparisons are made within the same job and establishment, and complaints are required to initiate comparisons. This is evidenced by the fact that such initiatives seem to have had no effect or only a small effect in decentralized, market-based wage determination systems such as in Canada and the United States. This also highlights the fact that wage inequality within the same job and establishment is unlikely to be large.

The scope of conventional equal pay policies appears to be larger in systems where wage determination is more formalized. This is evidenced by the more substantial effect of equal pay legislation under the collective-bargaining system in the United Kingdom or the tribunal decree system of Australia. Such systems did not rely on complaints and they could deal with wage differentials that occurred across occupations and establishments. The larger effect of equal pay policies in such situations is also indirect evidence that pay differences across occupations and establishments are likely to be a more important source of wage inequality than are pay differences within the same occupation and establishment.

The more substantial positive effect of affirmative action initiatives in the United States also suggests the broader scope for policies that can deal with occupational segregation as well as pay differences across establishments (and hence also industries). This also can be taken as indirect evidence of the greater importance of wage differences across occupations, firms and industries (as opposed to within the same occupation and firm) as a source of inequality in pay between men and women.

The effect of facilitating policies in reducing pay inequality has not been comprehensively documented. However, given that factors outside the labour market (e.g. education, family responsibilities) are important determinants of the earnings gap, this suggests a large potential role for policies that can facilitate the labour market participation of women on a more equal basis to that of men. Such facilitating policies can include education policies, child-care and elder-care programmes and parental leave.

The potential scope of comparable worth policies, and the inferences that can be made about the implications of this for the sources of pay in-equality will be documented in subsequent chapters when comparable worth itself is analysed. Given the wide range of factors influencing the overall male-female earnings gap, no single policy initiative will be suffi-cient to close the gap. Equal pay, equal employment opportunity policies, and facilitating policies all have a role to play, as do comparable worth policies.

CONCEPT OF COMPARABLE WORTH

4

As indicated previously, comparable worth generally requires that male-dominated and female-dominated jobs within the same establishment receive equal pay for work of equal value, where the value of the job is determined by gender-neutral, objective procedures like job evaluation. In this chapter, the *conceptual* issues associated with the concept of comparable worth are discussed. The next chapter deals with the *practical* or procedural issues involved with the design, implementation and administration of comparable worth.

4.1   ASPECTS OF THE DEFINITION OF COMPARABLE WORTH

Male- and female-dominated jobs

As outlined in more detail later, in the United States and Canada comparable worth comparisons are often allowed only when comparisons are made between female-dominated and male-dominated jobs, where gender dominance is defined in terms of some proportion (e.g. 70 per cent or more) of either sex. The rationale is that jobs that are disproportionately occupied by women are undervalued precisely because they are female-dominated. While this may be the case, there is no reason why it should be a necessary condition for such undervaluation. It is distinctly possible, for example, for a job occupied by a woman to be undervalued even though she works in a male-dominated or a mixed occupation. This broader concept of comparable worth seems to be followed more in Europe, where the legislation does not usually specify that an individual female who makes a complaint must be in a female-dominated job and must make a comparison only with a male in a male-dominated job.

There is obviously nothing "magical" about a specific cut-off like 70 per cent. In fact, gender dominance of a specific job should be relative to the gender composition of the workforce. For example, gender dominance of 70 per cent may be appropriate in developed countries where 40 per cent or more of the workforce may be female. But a 70 per cent cut-off in developing countries, where only 10 per cent of the workforce may be female, would lead to few jobs being classified as female-dominated. As such, it may be necessary to define gender dominance in relative terms; for example, when the job contains twice the proportion of women as found in the overall workforce.

When comparisons are made between male-dominated and female-dominated *jobs*, it is jobs that are being compared and not the individual males and females who occupy a job. Job evaluation systems evaluate jobs and not people. For comparable worth purposes, jobs are defined as "a grouping of positions that warrant similar treatment in terms of compensation, recruitment and other human resource practices" (Weiner and Gunderson, 1990, p. 158). Individuals, of course, may bring forth a complaint; however, it is their job that should be evaluated and not the individual person. In procedures where all female-dominated jobs within an organization receive a comparable worth wage adjustment, the wage increase goes to males as well as females in the undervalued female-dominated jobs. Also, while the concept of a job tends to correspond to that of an occupation, it is the actual job content that matters, and not the occupational designation.

While *gender* domination is the conventional criteria, conceptually there is nothing inherent in the procedure to prevent it from being applied to other forms of discrimination, such as discrimination on the bases of race or age.

Comparisons within the same establishment

Conventionally, comparable worth involves comparisons within the same establishment. The rationale for this has seldom been clearly articulated. It could reflect the fact that, as discussed previously, inter-firm wage differentials, even for apparently the same work, can arise for a variety of reasons besides discrimination. It could also reflect practical considerations associated with the fact that different establishments tend to use different job evaluation schemes; however, a given establishment also often uses more than one job evaluation scheme, with different ones being employed in female-dominated and in male-dominated jobs. There is also nothing conceptually inappropriate about using the same job evaluation scheme across different companies; large organizations may well do so across different branch plants.

If the concept of comparable worth is deemed appropriate, there is nothing illogical about extending it to comparisons across different establishments. The restrictions to within the same establishment seem to have to do more with practical considerations and with the notion that within the same establishment, the same personnel policy tends to be involved;

hence employers are being judged with respect to the internal consistency of their own compensation policies.

Equal value

With respect to the "equal value" aspect of the concept of comparable worth, a strict interpretation of the phrase "equal pay for work of equal value" would require male-comparator jobs of equal (or substantially similar) value. Conceptually, however, there is nothing inappropriate about making comparisons when the jobs are not of *equal* value, as long as the appropriate adjustment is made to pay. That is, *if* (and this is the important consideration) the comparable worth concept of value is deemed appropriate, then there is nothing inappropriate about extending it to situations where the jobs are not of equal value but where the relationship between the value of the jobs can be established. Once the concept of comparable worth is deemed appropriate, then conceptually there is no reason why comparable has to mean equal, as opposed to comparable in some appropriate way. If, for example, a female-dominated job were found to be 80 per cent of the value (e.g. job evaluation point scores) of a male-dominated job, but only paid 60 per cent of the pay of the male-dominated job, then there is nothing inappropriate about applying comparable worth to raise the pay of the female-dominated job to 80 per cent of the pay of the male-dominated job. Proportionate pay for work of proportionate value is a logical extension of equal pay for work of equal value. It is the comparable worth concept of value that should be at issue, not its extension to situations where proportionate value can be established, even though strict equal value comparisons cannot be established.

4.2 COMPARABLE WORTH CONCEPT OF VALUE

Many of the previously discussed aspects of the definition of comparable worth highlighted that it is the concept of comparable worth itself that is at issue, and not the appropriateness of extending it to such situations as comparisons across groups other than women, or across establishments, or to situations where the value or worth of the job is not equal. Once the concept of comparable worth is deemed appropriate, then there is nothing illogical to extend it to these other situations. Hence, it is important to have a clear understanding of the concept of value implied by comparable worth, and to contrast that with the economic concept of value.

Comparable worth involves an administrative concept of the value of a job, as opposed to the economic one where the value of a job is determined by the interaction of the forces of supply and demand. The administrative concept substitutes job evaluation procedures for market forces as the appropriate mechanism for determining the value of a job.

The rationale is that market forces reflect discrimination (whether from employers, co-workers or customers) and that an alternative procedure is thereby merited for determining the appropriate pay in female-dominated jobs. The presumption is that gender-neutral job evaluation procedures can be used as a measure of the value of a job, and that this provides an appropriate criterion for determining pay.

The appropriateness of job evaluation procedures for determining pay is based in part on the fact that such procedures are used in private industry to determine the relative worth (e.g. job evaluation points) of many jobs. This is the case, especially for jobs within the internal labour market of the firm where the pay is determined by administrative procedures and historical relationships, more so than by market forces. That is, market forces are important for determining the pay of certain "port-of-entry" jobs where recruiting is commonly done from the external labour market. These market-determined rates are then used as "benchmarks" for establishing the relative pay of other jobs within the firms' internal labour market, and for which external market comparisons are less possible because the firm tends to fill these jobs from internal promotion and reallocations from within rather than from external recruiting. In essence, the job evaluation procedures that are used to establish pay when market forces are not readily available are used under comparable worth to establish pay when the market forces are deemed to yield unsatisfactory outcomes.

It has certainly been pointed out that this can be a misuse of job evaluation by extending it to an area where its use was not intended, and for which it was not designed. More fundamentally, however, comparable worth can be regarded as akin to the search for a "just price", a concept that is at best elusive without regard to the concepts of demand (what people are willing and able to pay for a service) and supply (what others are willing to accept to provide the service). The concept of value implied by comparable worth is akin to the concept of "value in use", a notion that there are some intrinsic, objective notions of value. This is in contrast to the economic concept of "value in exchange" whereby the value of something is determined by what people are willing and able to give up in exchange for the commodity or service. This difference is illustrated by the well-known "diamond-water" paradox, whereby diamonds have a high value in exchange but little value in use, while water has a high value in use but little value in exchange. This occurs, of course, because in most circumstances diamonds are relatively scarce and water is relatively abundant, with respect to the demands for each.

The paradox in the comparable worth area has often been illustrated when considering the job of translators. Presumably translators of different common languages have comparable worth in the sense of similar skill, effort, responsibility and working conditions. But in some localities there may be no need or effective demand for translators of particular languages that are never used in those localities. Should all translators be given the same pay if they have the same job evaluation points, even if their services are not needed? Similarly, in other countries there may be an extreme need for translators of particular languages. Should they not receive a wage premium to attract their services?

Comparable worth advocates tend to regard the market more as part of the problem than part of the solution. Most economists, in contrast, would try to harness the forces of the market to alleviate the effects of discrimination. For example, if male-dominated jobs tended to pay 20 per cent more than female-dominated jobs of the same value, and the measure of value truly was a measure of value to the firm, then there would be a strong economic incentive for the firm to replace the more expensive males with the less expensive females. This process would raise the demand for females (and hence their wages) and it would break down the occupational segregation of females into low-wage female-dominated jobs. Firms that did not follow this procedure of hiring at the lowest price would not survive in the long run, just as would be the case for firms that paid 20 per cent more for machinery and equipment that was of the same value to them as a less expensive piece of machinery. Even if transaction costs and male resistance or female reluctance inhibited this process from *eliminating* discriminatory wage differentials, it should work in the direction of *reducing* such wage differentials.

4.3   PROACTIVE OR COMPLAINTS BASED

With respect to enforcement, there are two basic models of comparable worth: proactive and complaints based. As the name implies, the complaints-based procedure requires a complaint before the process is initiated. Depending upon the particular legislative requirements, complaints may come from individuals, trade unions or even from an enforcement agency, perhaps after a random investigation or an audit of the firm.

Individual complaints

Individuals can be severely hampered in lodging a complaint because of the technical knowledge required in this area (discussed in the next chapter). Individuals may be inhibited by the threat of retribution, even if the legislation provides protection against such retribution. Individuals may also not have the full incentive to carry through a complaint because they have to bear the cost of the process and yet the benefits of their settlement may spill over to other individuals in similar circumstances. Fearing the precedent that such settlements may establish, employers may devote an inordinate amount of resources to win their case, even though the benefit to them of settling that particular case may not be large.

Complaints-based systems can also be costly in terms of time and resources, especially if they become legalistic. They can also foster an adversarial approach to social problem solving. While this may be necessary, and indeed effective, such an adversarial climate may also carry over to other dimensions of the employment relationship. This consequence may be considered negative at a time when cooperative solutions to labour management are being sought. Furthermore, the long-run effectiveness of the policy is likely to be enhanced if it is jointly designed and agreed upon by the parties who have to live with the arrangement, rather than it being imposed by an outside party in the process of settling a complaint.

Enforcement agencies

Enforcement agencies can be empowered to lodge complaints, as well as responding to the complaints of individuals. They could do so, for example, after a random investigation or a routine audit of a firm. Such enforcement agencies could specialize in pay equity issues, or they could be responsible for such issues as part of their other mandates such as general employment standards.

Such agencies can have the technical and informational expertise that is important in this area. They need not be concerned with reprisals or with creating an adversarial environment; in fact, they can deflect the adversarial aspects towards themselves and away from the workplace. The effectiveness of such administrative agencies, however, can be dependent upon the budget and resources allocated to them, although this dependency may be deemed appropriate if it is considered desirable that the application of such laws reflect the current political climate.

Unions

Unions can be a viable mechanism for carrying through complaints because they can have the technical expertise which is so important in this area, and they can protect employees against retribution. As indicated subsequently, in the countries where comparable worth has been most advanced, unions have been an important vehicle in that process.

Unions could of course bargain for comparable worth even if there were no legislative requirements in that area. However, this would most likely mean that something else would have to be given up in the inevitable trade-offs that are involved in collective bargaining. Unions may regard this as inappropriate on the grounds that they should not have to trade to obtain certain basic rights, such as a workplace that is free of discrimination. Having such rights provided by broad-based legislation means that the cost implications do not just fall on unionized employers, which otherwise could jeopardize their own competitive position as well as the jobs of union members. Unions also want to try to keep pay-equity bargaining separate from regular collective bargaining, in part to reduce the likelihood that pay-equity settlements will come out of the funds that would otherwise go to workers as part of collective bargaining.

While unions can be a viable mechanism for enforcing pay equity, they can create another set of problems in the process. There is always the possibility that such issues may be bargained away, especially if women are not a viable force within the union, either at the rank-and-file or leadership level. Depending upon the nature of the bargaining process, comparable worth may get caught up in the adversarial aspects of such bargaining. It may also get caught up in serving other agendas besides the needs of those subject to discrimination.

4.4 PROACTIVE APPLICATION

In part, because of the problems associated with complaints-based systems, advocates of comparable worth have emphasized the need for what is often termed a proactive approach. Such an approach would require employers to have a comparable worth procedure in place, whether or not there has been a complaint or prima facie evidence of wage discrimination.

This proactive approach in the comparable worth area is akin to the affirmative-action approach to equal employment opportunity legislation. That is, rather than relying on a complaint to activate an investigation of discrimination in hiring or promotion, the affirmative-action approach requires employers to have an affirmative-action plan in place, whether or not there has been a complaint or prima facie evidence of employment discrimination.

The rationale behind proactive comparable worth is similar to that of affirmative action. Discrimination may be systemic or an unintended by-product of other actions within the workplace as well as society at large. As such, it is not sufficient to rely on complaints or minor tinkering to provide redress. Policies must be put in place that alter the fundamental character of the hiring and promotion decision (in the case of affirmative action) and the compensation policy (in the case of comparable worth).

STEPS INVOLVED IN APPLYING COMPARABLE WORTH

5

The importance of the practical issues of design, implementation and administration of comparable worth have been recognized in the literature on the topic.[1] There is, however, less agreement about the proper way to deal with them. Unfortunately, much of the debate occurs at the implementation stage itself, with different parties favouring procedures on the basis of how it affects their own particular position, when what is needed is debate and analysis on general principles that are not tied to any particular implementation case. These generic principles can then be applied in general terms to the various implementation steps: (1) identifying male- and female-dominated jobs; (2) determining the value of the jobs, usually by a gender-neutral job evaluation scheme; (3) determining the relationship between pay and value; and (4) adjusting the pay in the undervalued female-dominated jobs. In this chapter, each of these steps will be discussed in turn, emphasizing the assumptions, pitfalls, biases and subjectiveness involved in each stage. In the next chapter, other design and implementation issues are discussed, especially pertaining to the design of the legislation itself.

The emphasis in this chapter is on the proactive application of comparable worth within an organization, rather than how it may be utilized in a specific complaint by a female job incumbent. Many of the issues, however, are relevant to the situations of individual complaints as well as to the broader proactive application.

5.1 IDENTIFYING MALE- AND FEMALE-DOMINATED JOBS

The first step in applying pay equity involves the identification of male-dominated and female-dominated jobs within the establishment. The rationale is that female-dominated jobs tend to be systematically undervalued, and that male-dominated jobs provide the best comparison group for establishing the appropriate value for the female-dominated jobs.

Procedures for establishing gender dominance

Gender dominance of a particular job is usually established by a quantitative measure such as 70 per cent male for male-dominated jobs and 70 per cent female for female-dominated jobs. The implicit assumption is that jobs that do not meet those cut-offs are sufficiently mixed so as not to be subject to serious discrimination, or at least discrimination that can best be addressed by comparable worth. Obviously, there is an element of subjectiveness to the cut-off; however, some criteria must be used as long as the principle is to eliminate the systematic undervaluation of female-dominated jobs.

The trade-off is that a more stringent cut-off (e.g. 80 per cent gender dominated) would be more reflective of the effect of stronger gender dominance; however, it would provide redress to fewer groups. Also, it may yield fewer male-dominated comparator groups. A broader cut-off (e.g. 55 per cent gender dominated) would provide redress to more female-dominated jobs and would provide more male-dominated comparator groups; however, this would come at the expense of not focusing on the more serious cases of gender dominance. While the total adjustments may be larger because more groups are involved, they would be smaller on a per-recipient basis because the comparisons are being made across more mixed jobs where presumably the wage gap would be smaller.

As discussed previously, different cut-offs may be appropriate, depending upon the overall percentage of the workforce that is female. Different cut-offs could also be required for male-dominated as opposed to female-dominated jobs. For example, given that males tend to dominate the workforce as a whole, a higher cut-off may be allowed on male-dominated jobs before they are considered male-dominated. In Canada, for example, both the provinces of Ontario and New Brunswick define a job to be female-dominated if it is 60 per cent or more female, but male-dominated if it is 70 per cent or more male.

Different cut-offs could also be required depending upon the size of the organization. For example, in the federal jurisdiction of Canada, the cut-offs for male-dominated jobs are 70 per cent or more for groups of less than 100 employees, 60 per cent for groups of 100 to 500 employees, and 55 per cent or more for groups of more than 500 employees. The rationale for the sliding scale is to ensure that different group sizes have the same degree of statistical certainty that the composition of the group is not due to random chance (Juriansz, 1987b, p. 674). For example, in a small establishment, a higher cut-off (e.g. 70 per cent as opposed to 55 per cent male) makes it less likely that the group would be predominantly male due to random chance.

Problems and possible solutions

There are various problems and pitfalls associated with the criteria of gender dominance, and in varying degrees solutions have been suggested. For example, employers may try to redefine the job classes so as to minimize the number of female-dominated jobs, or they may try to change the numbers in particular classes so as to just fall below the particular cut-off (e.g. shifting some females out of a female-dominated job class so as to change it from 70 per cent female to 68 per cent female). To a certain degree this can be dealt with by looking at the recent history of the gender dominance of the job (termed historical incumbency) or by subjective criteria such as the gender stereotyping of the work.[2] Obviously, elements of subjectivity can be involved in this process, and procedures must be established for ultimately settling any disputes. Another problem is raised in some developing countries where women comprise only a small percentage of the non-agricultural labour force (often only 10 per cent or so) which implies that even a relatively low criterion for defining female-dominated jobs of say 60 per cent may rarely be found.

Smaller establishments especially may have too few job incumbents to make viable comparisons. This can be dealt with in a variety of ways, all of which have their own problems. The definition of gender dominance can be broadened to provide a larger "catchment", and this could even vary by the number of persons in the job classification. A minimum number of job incumbents could also be required before the job is included in the comparable worth process.[3]

The use of specific criteria for defining female dominance can also create inequities in that fairly similar groups may be treated quite differently. If a 70 per cent cut-off is used, for example, persons in jobs that are 71 per cent female-dominated may receive substantial wage adjustments (e.g. 20 per cent or more), while those in jobs that are 69 per cent female-dominated may receive no adjustment at all. This inequity can create resentment since it is unlikely that the degree of discrimination is substantially different between those two situations.

Expanding the definition of female dominance (e.g. to 60 per cent or more female) reduces the number of such situations but it does so at the expense of giving adjustments to jobs that are only marginally female-dominated. Large numbers of males will also receive those adjustments (e.g. up to 40 per cent of the job incumbents). There will always be a margin as long as a specific proportion is used to define gender dominance (in this example, the margin is simply displaced to those in jobs that are just under the cut-off of 60 per cent female dominated).

The severity of the problem *may* be reduced somewhat by the fact that the wage gap may be smaller for jobs that are more mixed and that therefore approach the cut-off. This is so because those jobs by definition have more males and for that reason may be more highly paid. In such circumstances, persons who fall just outside the cut-off may compare themselves with those just above the cut-off where the wage gap is smallest. But there is no guarantee that this is the case.

Some ad hoc procedures

In order to minimize such inequities, and the morale problems that may ensue, the organization may follow certain ad hoc procedures. For example, attempts may be made to regroup the otherwise marginal job classes so that they are either clearly in the female-dominated classes or clearly in the mixed ones, with the result that close comparisons are less likely. Or, for those groups just under the cut-off, the firm may grant larger wage increases through the normal channels of collective bargaining or the firm's compensation policy. Obviously, this has cost implications, and just at the time that the pay equity increases are being absorbed. Alternatively, the pay equity increases may not be widely publicized, although this is at the cost of people being unaware that they are receiving redress. When the comparable worth procedure is part of collective bargaining, the union may focus its attention on winning other quid pro quos for those groups who marginally miss out on pay equity adjustments, although it is not obvious that such quid pro quos can be targeted in that direction.

5.2 DETERMINING THE VALUE OF THE JOBS VIA JOB EVALUATION[4]

Once the gender-dominated jobs are established, the next step in the application of comparable worth is to determine the "value" of the jobs so that comparisons can be made between jobs of equal value. Essentially, this is done through gender-neutral job evaluation procedures, although in theory less formal procedures could be used. For example, in a collective bargaining procedure or a complaints-based procedure, the parties could simply mutually agree upon the appropriate comparator jobs based on an implicit understanding of what jobs are of comparable value. In situations where wages are fixed by decree or set by tribunals or arbitrators, it is possible for them to award higher amounts to female-dominated jobs, and to label these as comparable worth adjustments. In general, however, the strict application of comparable worth involves the use of formal job evaluation procedures to determine the worth or value of the jobs. In fact, job evaluation is a key ingredient of comparable worth.

Basic job evaluation procedures

There are a host of job evaluation procedures ranging from simple rankings of jobs, to the classification of jobs into common job grades or to the use of job evaluation point scores. They all tend to involve a set of generic ingredients, many of which have to be modified or adapted to be applied to the area of comparable worth.

Job evaluation starts with a job description that should be an accurate description of the essential ingredients of the job. In the application to comparable worth it is essential that the job descriptions describe the tasks that are actually performed since it is the actual tasks that matter and not a hypothetical set of tasks that are involved in an outmoded or inaccurate job description. Also, the essential or main tasks are at issue, not some occasional tasks that may be performed, albeit the latter may be relevant if the ability to occasionally deal with an unpredictable set of circumstances is an important ingredient of the job.

The job description can come from any number of sources, a procedure termed job analysis. The sources can include the job incumbents, their supervisors or job analysts in the human resource staff or from outside consultants. Information can come from questionnaires, interviews, direct observation or job content analysis.

Once an accurate job analysis and job description is made the jobs are then evaluated. In the comparable worth application this is a crucial step because it is essentially how the value or "worth" of the jobs are established. This is often done by a committee of managers and supervisors, sometimes with professional outside assistance. Employees may be made members of the committee to provide information and to facilitate credibility. If a union is involved it would usually represent the employees. In some circumstances, joint labour management committees may be required by law.

The job evaluation procedure essentially involves determining the key ingredients of the job in terms of factors such as skill, effort, responsibility and working conditions, termed compensable factors. In the point factor job evaluation schemes, these factors are assigned points within a predetermined range. The range may differ across the factors, which implicitly allows them to have different weights. For example, skill may have a range of 10 to 30 points, and responsibility a range of 30 to 60 points, which implicitly allows responsibility to be two to three times as important as skill. As well, explicit weights may be assigned to each compensable factor. For example, skill may be assigned a weight of 20 per cent, effort 30 per cent, responsibility 40 per cent and working conditions 10 per cent. The weighted point scores are then usually summed to get a total job evaluation point score. This is the value or worth of the job.

Potential gender biases in job evaluation

Obviously, there is potential scope for gender bias to enter each and every step in the job evaluation procedure. The job analysis that goes into the job description tends to be done by supervisors, managers and job incumbents. Since supervisors and managers tend to be male, the potential for gender stereotyping is present. For example, occasional tasks such as heavy lifting may enter as essential functions in the male-dominated jobs, while occasional unpleasant tasks done in the female-dominated jobs may not enter as essential functions, especially if they are regarded as jobs typically done by women, perhaps as extensions of their work done in the household. Even the female job incumbents themselves may downplay such tasks.

In the job evaluation procedure itself gender biases may occur especially because the parties may not clearly distinguish evaluating the job as opposed to the individuals involved in the job. The committees themselves may have the same gender biases that typify the rest of society. Even when women are on the committees, there may be a selection bias in that they are more likely to be supervisory or senior employees, and they may have arrived at that position because they themselves were not subject to discrimination. As such, they may not perceive discrimination in other jobs.

Clearly, there is ample scope for gender bias to permeate each and every step in the job evaluation procedure. Since that procedure is part and parcel of the personnel and human resource policies that gave rise to systemic discrimination in the first place, there is no reason to believe that it will be free of gender bias, unless conscious steps are taken in that direction. Suggested steps include:

(1) using multiple sources (e.g. supervisors, encumbents, committees) and a standard format that is sensitive to factors typically missed in women's jobs to collect job information;

(2) training of job encumbents, supervisors and job analysts in comparable worth procedures; and

(3) writing job descriptions in a standard and consistent format, especially across male- and female-dominated jobs (Weiner and Gunderson, 1990, p. 37).

5.3 ESTABLISHING RELATIONSHIP BETWEEN PAY AND POINTS

Once the value of the job is established via job evaluation, the next step typically involves relating the value of the job to the pay in the job. In the conventional cases of factor point job evaluation procedures, this involves estimating the relationship between pay and job evaluation points. If pay and points are related by definition (i.e. the organization follows a practice of "pay for point"), then the relationship is already established and does not have to be estimated. Comparable worth procedures are still relevant because they would still be needed to ensure that the definition of the relationship between pay and points was the same for male and female jobs.

There are a variety of ways of estimating the relationship between pay and points, each with their own properties and therefore explicit or implicit assumptions. In many cases, it is not so much that one method is correct and the other incorrect. Rather, they have different properties and assumptions. In such circumstances it is best to make these explicit so that the choice of procedure can be made on the bases of which properties and assumptions are most consistent with achieving the goals of pay equity in the most effective fashion.

Scatter diagrams

The relationship between pay and job evaluation point scores can be depicted by a simple scatter diagram with pay on the vertical axes and job evaluation scores on the horizontal axes (figure 5.1). The points in the diagram would indicate the pay that is associated with the job evaluation score for each job. The scatter of points for the male-dominated jobs will typically lie above the scatter for the female-dominated jobs, indicating that male-dominated jobs tend to be paid more than female-dominated jobs of the same job evaluation score. They also are typically above and to the right of the female-dominated jobs, since there are often a large number of male-dominated jobs at the higher end of the scores, and few at the lower end of job evaluation scores. The latter indicates a problem, discussed subsequently, of having no male comparator jobs of the same job evaluation score for some of the female-dominated jobs (i.e. over the dashed-line segment extending to the left from the male pay line).

The relationship between pay and job evaluation scores can be summarized by simply drawing a male pay line through the scatter of points for the male-dominated jobs, and a female pay line through the scatter of points for the female-dominated jobs (termed "eye-balling" the data). Since substantial magnitudes of money can be involved in the wage adjustment steps, however, it is usually best to estimate the line by more rigorous methods such as regression procedures. Such procedures also more explicitly lay out the properties and assumptions of the estimated relationship between pay and job evaluation scores.

Regression procedures

In regression analysis, pay in each job (the dependent variable) is typically regressed on the job evaluation point score (the independent variable) of each job. Separate pay lines are typically estimated for the male-dominated jobs (male pay line) and for the female-dominated jobs (female pay line) within the organization. The estimated regression coefficient, or slope of each pay line, indicates how pay is increased for each unit increase in the job evaluation point score. It is the implicit or "shadow price" of each job evaluation score.

While a formal, rigorous analysis of the properties of regression procedures are beyond the scope of this study, a number of properties are

Figure 5.1   Male and female pay lines

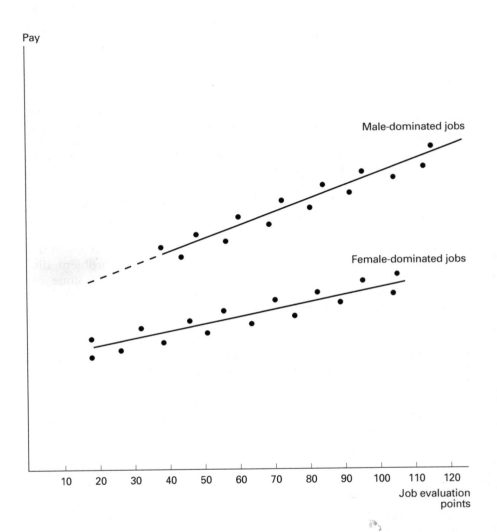

worth mentioning, with particular emphasis on their implications for comparable worth analysis.

Number of observations for estimating pay lines

The accuracy or precision of estimating the pay lines will depend in part on the number of observations showing the relationship between pay and points. There is no obvious minimum number of observations required before the pay lines can be deemed to provide a "good fit" to the data. The precision with which the pay lines can be estimated will depend in part on the pay policy of the organization. An organization that ties its pay to the job evaluation points will pay according to the pay line, and the "scatter" of points will be on or near the pay line. The pay lines may still differ between male and female jobs (in which case, comparable worth does not prevail), but the scatter of points will be close to each pay line. In such organizations fewer observations are necessary to accurately estimate the pay lines than in organizations that do not follow a policy of pay for points, and the scatter of points is widely dispersed around each pay line.

Functional form of pay lines

The estimated pay lines could have any number of functional forms to depict the relationship between pay and points. The pay lines could be linear (e.g. figure 5.1), in which case the relationship between pay and points is the same throughout the range of the pay line. This implicitly assumes, for example, that an *additional* job evaluation point is worth the same at a job evaluation score of 100 as it is at a score of 200. This may or may not be reasonable, depending upon how the job evaluation scores were constructed in the first place.

The pay lines could be non-linear, which would allow the relationship between pay and points to differ depending upon the level of the points. Separate piece-wise regression lines could also be estimated over different ranges of the job evaluation scores. This could be appropriate if, for example, the data points themselves showed such a relationship to exist. It is not uncommon, for example, for the male pay line to flatten out at the high end of the job evaluation scores, so that additional points in that range are not associated with large absolute increases in pay (Michael et al., 1989, p. 203).

It is extremely difficult to state in advance whether any particular functional form is "better" than another, in the absence of any theoretical reason as to the appropriate relationship between pay and points. If the job evaluation scheme is set up so that a given point is expected to be "worth" the same whatever the level of the score, then a linear relationship is appropriate. Otherwise using the relationship that best "fits" the data may be appropriate, although complex functional forms have problems of not being easily understood. Trade-offs may be involved between simplicity and best-fits or other criteria. Alternative functional forms may be tried, with choices having to be made only if there are large differences. However, this can create problems of appearing to manipulate the data.

Separate scores as regressors

Adding the separate job evaluation scores for each of the compensable factors implicitly assumes that they have the same weight. This may be reasonable if the job evaluation procedure was designed with that constraint in mind.

An alternative procedure would be to enter the separate scores for each compensable factors as separate regressors. If there were four compensable factors (skill, effort, responsibility and working conditions) then there would be four separate regressors. The resulting regression coefficients would indicate the weight or shadow price the organization attaches to each of these compensable factors. Statistical tests could be utilized to see if these weights in fact are similar, in which case they could then be summed to get a total job evaluation score. If they are not similar, then it may be appropriate to use the separate weights to adjust the pay in the female-dominated jobs.

Outliers

Conventional regression procedures provide a "best fit" to the scatter of pay and points, in that the line will minimize the sum of squared deviations about the line. That property by itself has no obvious implication for comparable worth, except that the slope of the line will be heavily influenced by "outliers" or large deviations about the line (because the deviations are squared before their sum is minimized). Thus, for example, a male-dominated job that has unusually high pay, given its job evaluation score, will have a disproportionately large influence on the slope of the male pay line (i.e. on the relationship between pay and points in male-dominated jobs).

If this is considered an undesirable property, then consideration should be given to the treatment of "outliers" in the data. Options could include: omitting the outliers altogether on the grounds that they are not representative cases; reassessing the job evaluation procedure that gave rise to their score; or examining their pay to see if some component represents an unusual circumstance that would not be considered discriminatory. Whatever procedure is followed, it would be important to ensure that it did not impart any gender bias.

Weighting

Since the different jobs being evaluated have different numbers of incumbents, it seems appropriate to use weighted least squares regression procedures so that a higher weight is given to observations (i.e. jobs with their corresponding pay and points) with a large number of incumbents. This does not violate the principle that it is jobs and not people that are being compared, because the jobs are simply being weighted by the number of incumbents.

Intercept

Conventional regression procedures have an intercept term when pay lines are estimated. In the comparable worth application, this implies that some pay is appropriate even if there is no value to the job in terms of job evaluation points. This seems inappropriate, unless the pay could be regarded as a minimum base amount that is awarded and then augmented as job evaluation points are accumulated. The intercept term in the regression procedure also has other properties, such as ensuring that the regression line passes through the mean of the data. This, in turn implies that the average pay in the organization will equal the pay received by a person in a job with the average job evaluation point score.

Identical slopes

In estimating separate pay lines for male-dominated and female-dominated jobs, the issue remains as to whether the pay lines should be constrained to have the same slope.[5] In such circumstances, the female pay line would be parallel to the male pay line and below it, assuming the female-dominated jobs are paid less than male-dominated jobs. Identical slopes imply that male- and female-dominated jobs receive the same *increment* in pay for the same increase in job evaluation points.

Constraining the slopes to be the same in the estimation of the male and female pay lines, ensures that the pay adjustment will be the same at all levels of the job evaluation scores. This may be desirable if different adjustments could create problems of internal equity. However, it comes at the expense of giving the same adjustment even though some female-dominated jobs may be more undervalued then others, relative to the male-dominated jobs. For that reason, it seems more appropriate to "let the data speak for itself" and allow the slopes to differ if in fact the relationship between pay and points is different for male- and female-dominated jobs.

Percentage female as a regressor

Comparable worth should eliminate the relationship between pay and the gender composition of a job. The gender composition of a job can be captured by including a variable representing the percentage female of the job in the estimating equation relating pay to job evaluation points. The estimated regression coefficient would indicate the effect, on pay, of a one-unit increase in the proportion of the job occupants who are female. A statistically significant negative coefficient would indicate that the female composition of the job has a significant negative effect on wages in the job. Comparable worth wage adjustments could be required until that effect is eliminated within the organization (i.e. the coefficient on percentage female is zero).

This could be done on all jobs within the organization, or it could be done only on the gender-dominated jobs as is the case in conventional comparable worth applications. It could be done on a composite pay line that included both male- and female-dominated jobs, or it could be done on separate male and female pay lines. In the latter case, it would ensure that even within male-dominated and female-dominated jobs, the gender composition would have no impact on pay.

5.4   APPROPRIATE WAGE ADJUSTMENT

In the pay-line procedures, once the pay lines are estimated, the next step in applying comparable worth involves determining the appropriate procedure for adjusting wages to ensure equal pay for work of equal value. A variety of options are available, each with their own properties and assumptions. A more detailed illustration of those options is given in Weiner and Gunderson (1990, pp. 76-89).

Pay line-to-pay line

One procedure is to adjust the female pay line to the male pay line. In figure 5.1, this would entail raising the pay in each of the female-dominated jobs (i.e. points around the female pay line) by an amount equal to the difference between the male and female pay lines at the job evaluation score for that female-dominated job. If the slopes are different, this will imply a different magnitude of wage awards at different job evaluation scores. The male pay line is taken as the nondiscriminatory norm. Whatever factors that determine the relationship between pay and points in the male-dominated jobs are simply applied to the female-dominated jobs. This is termed a policy capturing approach in that it simply captures the policy that applies to wage determination in male-dominated jobs, and extends that policy to female-dominated jobs.

The line-to-line approach leaves the deviations about both the male and female lines intact. The rationale is that these are simply random deviations since they exist about both the male- and female-dominated jobs. Only the systematic differences in pay between male- and female-dominated jobs of the same value are removed. This does imply, however, that some female-dominated jobs will remain undervalued about the male pay line since they will still be below the male pay line, just as they earlier were below the female pay line. Similarly, some will be overvalued since they will be above the male pay line, just as they previously were above the female pay line.

Of course, there will still be deviations of male jobs about the male pay line, unless the organization eliminates them as a conscious policy of internal equity. This would be difficult, however, because the legislation would usually require that pay will not fall in any jobs as a result of pay equity. This means that the organization could only raise the pay in the male jobs that were below the male pay line, without lowering the pay in those that were above the line, and this has obvious cost implications.

Point-to-pay line

An alternative procedure would be to raise the pay in each female-dominated job to the male pay line. In the previous figure 5.1, this would entail raising each point around the female pay line to the male pay line. This would eliminate both random deviations in pay (i.e. about the female pay line) as well as systematic differences in pay (i.e. between the male and female pay lines). It would still leave the random deviations in pay of male-dominated jobs about the male pay line, and in that sense there would be an asymmetry of treatment.

The rationale for this procedure is that if female-dominated jobs are not to be undervalued, then they should be raised to the male pay line since that would imply equal pay for work of equal value. That is, they would be paid the same as the male-dominated jobs of the same value.

This assumes, however, that to eliminate undervaluation it is necessary to eliminate both random undervaluation (i.e. differences about the female pay line) and systematic undervaluation (i.e. differences between the male and female pay lines). However, random deviations about the female pay line do not reflect discrimination because they are occurring *within* the female-dominated jobs, just as they also occur within the male-dominated jobs. Such random deviations are the result of normal deviations in pay that exist under job evaluation schemes for jobs of the same value. They are the subject matter of internal equity if the firm chooses to eliminate or reduce such deviations; they are not the subject matter of pay equity which deals with systematic differences in pay between male- and female-dominated jobs of the same value. Since such random deviations in pay are not eliminated within the male-dominated jobs, and since they prevailed within the female-dominated jobs prior to pay equity, it seems inappropriate to eliminate them through pay equity.

Point-to-point adjustment

An alternative procedure that does not involve the estimation of pay lines is a point-to-point adjustment whereby the pay in the female-dominated job is adjusted to the pay of the specific male-dominated job of equal or comparable value as determined by job evaluation. In figure 5.1, this would entail raising each point around the female pay line to the point around the male pay line that has the closest job evaluation score to the female job. This is implicitly the procedure that is used, for example, in complaints-based systems where a female job incumbent is required to find a male comparator job of equal or comparable value. It can also be used, however, in proactive systems where all of the male- and female-dominated jobs in the organization are evaluated, and given a job evaluation score.

This procedure does require an algorithm or decision rule for situations where there is more than one male-dominated job of the same value, or where there are no male-dominated jobs of the same value. Obvious possibilities are the average pay of the male-dominated jobs if there are more than one of the same value. In the case of no specific male comparator of the same value, an average of the "surrounding" male jobs could be used, perhaps weighted in accordance with their closeness to the female-dominated jobs, essentially determining the "pay for points" in the surrounding male-dominated jobs and applying that to the points of the female-dominated jobs.

In the province of Ontario in Canada, such a job-to-job comparator approach tends to be utilized. If there is no male comparator group of the same value, then the legislation requires comparisons to be made with the highest paying male job of the next lowest job evaluation score. If there is more than one male comparator job of the same value, then the lowest paying male job is used. Obviously, this can create the potential for strategic behaviour on the part of the organization to structure comparator jobs so as to minimize the adjustment that is necessary. It also highlights the point that avoiding the technical requirements of regression lines still leaves a set of technical requirements with respect to the choice of comparator groups.

The point-to-point adjustment procedure can have considerable variability since the deviations around what would otherwise be a female pay line are matched to the deviations around what would otherwise be a male pay line. That is, there is no "smoothing" of the data through the use of regression lines. In that sense, the procedure eliminates what would be the systematic differences in discrimination between male and female-dominated jobs (i.e. differences in the pay lines) as well as the random differences in pay (i.e. deviations about the pay lines). This could mean that some very large awards may occur (if what would be a large negative deviation in female pay were matched to a large positive deviation in male pay). These could co-exist with some very small adjustments (if what would be a large positive deviation in female pay were matched to a large negative deviation in male pay). To the extent that large differences in the awards within the female-dominated jobs within the same organization are considered undesirable because invidious comparisons are then set up, this could be considered an undesirable feature of the point-to-point wage adjustment procedure.

Adjustments to the average pay line

Instead of adjusting the pay in undervalued female-dominated jobs to a male pay line, it is possible to adjust them to an aggregate pay line of both male- and female-dominated jobs. This would be possible whether a line-to-line or point-to-line procedure is used. That is, the reference line would be the aggregate average pay line and not the pay line from male-dominated jobs. If, in fact, both the male-dominated and female-dominated jobs were adjusted to the aggregate pay line, then this procedure essentially would be one of attaining full internal equity within the organization by having all jobs paid according to the pay for points relationship of the estimated pay line.

The problem with this approach of adjusting to the average pay line when applied to pay equity is that the aggregate pay line that is used as the non-discriminatory norm includes the female-dominated jobs that are allegedly subject to discrimination. After the adjustment, the male-dominated jobs could still disproportionately lie above the new pay line, while the female-dominated jobs would be on the pre-adjustment aggregate pay line. Although the latter could still be disproportionately below a new aggregate pay line if one were estimated, in such circumstances, the female-dominated jobs would still be undervalued.

The only way in which the female-dominated jobs would not lie below a newly estimated pay line is if the overvalued male-dominated jobs were also brought down to the aggregate pay line. Such a procedure would be consistent with achieving internal equity; however, it could not occur under legislated pay equity adjustments since such laws invariably have the requirement that wages will not be reduced in any job in order to achieve pay equity.

While adjusting to an aggregate pay line would still leave the female-dominated jobs undervalued (assuming the male-dominated jobs were not brought down to the average pay line) the adjustment would be in the right direction of achieving comparable worth (that is, the unequal pay gap would be reduced). In that case, such an adjustment procedure could be a way of phasing in the adjustment to comparable worth. After the first adjustment, a new average pay line could be estimated and an additional adjustment made. This process could continue until the gap was reduced to near zero.

Variants of previous approaches

Numerous variants of the previous approaches are also possible. For example, in the line-to-line approach, female-dominated jobs that are already above the male pay line could be exempt from the common adjustment that goes to other female-dominated jobs. "Corridors" could be established about the male pay line or an aggregated pay line with adjustments to the corridor going only to those jobs that are sufficiently undervalued to be below the corridor. The corridor could be an absolute amount of pay, or a percentage figure (e.g. 5 per cent below male pay line).

5.5   CONCLUDING OBSERVATIONS ON IMPLEMENTATION STEPS

Clearly, there are a variety of issues that are involved in each and every step in the implementation of comparable worth within an organization. For most of these issues, difficult technical procedures are involved, often requiring knowledge from a variety of disciplines or areas: statistics; job evaluation; human resource management; labour relations; law; psychology; and economics. Trade-offs may well be involved between procedures that are technically correct, and that are more readily understood and hence more likely to be accepted and perceived by the parties as fair.

In many circumstances, however, there are not technically correct procedures as opposed to different procedures with different properties and implicit or explicit assumption. In these cases it is important to outline the properties of the procedures and the trade-offs that are involved. This will facilitate the choice of appropriate procedures on the basis of their generic properties, rather than on their results in any particular application. If comparable worth is to become more widely adopted, it is imperative that there be greater understanding and agreement on the appropriate steps in its application.

Notes

[1] Pierson, Shallcross-Koziara and Johannesson, 1984, p. 118; Acker, 1989, p. 106; Abbott, 1989, p. 20; McDermott, 1991, p. 22; Treiman and Hartmann, 1981, p. 84; Remick, 1984, p. xi; Gunderson, 1989b, p. 214.

[2] In Canada, for example, in addition to a quantitative cut-off of 70 per cent for male dominance and 60 per cent for female dominance, the province of Ontario has two additional criteria for the determination of gender dominance: the historical incumbency of the job; and the gender stereotype of the work involved. In the province of New Brunswick, where comparable worth is to be negotiated through the unions, the criteria for gender dominance can also be negotiated, taking into account such factors as historical incumbency.

[3] In the provinces of Manitoba and New Brunswick in Canada, where comparable worth is implemented through the collective bargaining process, a minimum of ten incumbents is required before the job is included in the comparable worth process.

[4] The use of job evaluation in comparable worth, and the potential biases that may exist, are discussed in Acker (1987, 1989), Ad Hoc Working Group on Pay Equity and Job Classification Sys-

tems (1981), Arvey (1986), Schwab and Wichern (1983), Steinberg (1986), Treiman (1979), and Weiner and Gunderson (1990), as well as in various articles in Hartman (1985), Livernash (1984), Lowe and Wittig (1989), and Remick (1984).

[5] Constraining the slopes to be equal is the same as estimating a common relationship between pay and points for both sexes, and including a dummy variable for the female-dominated jobs. The estimated coefficient for that variable would indicate the comparable worth wage gap.

ADDITIONAL DESIGN AND IMPLEMENTATION ISSUES

6

The previous chapter dealt with a number of practical and technical issues associated with the application of comparable worth legislation through the four basic steps in its application. In this chapter, additional design and implementation issues are discussed as they arise in the more general application of comparable worth.

6.1 ALLOWABLE EXCEPTIONS

Comparable worth legislation often allows for wage differences to prevail across jobs of equal value, and for these differences not to be considered as discriminatory, providing they reflect certain factors that are considered as "allowable exceptions". These factors are generally regarded as giving rise to legitimate wage differences, even though the jobs may be of equal value as determined by job evaluation procedures. In general, the allowable exceptions refer to the jobs, since that is the appropriate unit for comparable worth comparisons, although at times they can refer to exemptions for specific individual incumbents.

Weiner and Gunderson (1990, p. 112) list, in roughly descending order of their prevalence, the main exemptions that are allowed in a number of different Canadian jurisdictions that have adopted proactive pay equity legislation:

(i) **merit** – providing objective, non-discriminatory, performance appraisal systems are used, and the same principles are applied to the male-dominated and female-dominated jobs;

(ii) **seniority** – where it has been part of the regular compensation system;

(iii) **skill** or labour shortage – providing they are temporary wage premiums paid to reduce certain skill shortages or labour shortages;

(iv) **red-circling** – where the wages paid in the male-dominated comparator jobs are temporarily high for unusual reasons such as the downgrading of the job (with the incumbent's wages being frozen until the wages in the lower-valued jobs catch up), or because the employee is reassigned to a lower job but allowed to keep the wages of their former job (again with the wages being frozen until the wages in the lower valued jobs catch up);

(v) **temporary training assignments** – where the worker is temporarily assigned to a job with a high training or employee development programme, and the employee effectively "pays" for some of that training by taking a lower wage during the training period;

(vi) **geographic differences** – regional wage differences may be allowed across jobs of the same job evaluation value within the same organization with different regional operations, providing they reflect established regional wage policies, for example, to compensate for differences in the cost of living;

(vii) **experience** – providing the experience is relevant to carrying out the job;

(viii) **productivity** – as measured by the quantity of goods or services produced;

(ix) **overtime** – wage premiums that reflect overtime are allowed even though they may reflect higher pay for the same work done during the regular work-day;

(x) **Bargaining strength** – after pay equity has been achieved, unequal pay for equal work may resurface providing it reflects differences in bargaining strength across the jobs of equal value.

To reduce the potential for abuse, many of the allowable exemptions have other stringent conditions attached to them. For example, in one jurisdiction that allows wage premiums in male-dominated jobs providing they exist to cover a skill shortage, the employer must show that the same wage premium prevails relative to other male-dominated jobs that do not have a skill shortage.

Many of the allowable exemptions can come very close to violating the spirit if not the specific intent of comparable worth legislation. This is the case, for example, with respect to the exemptions for seniority and experience, although they may be proxies for the skill component of the job. If so, however, that should be captured in the skill component of the job evaluation procedure. Similarly, wage differences arising from productivity differences are consistent with wage differences reflecting variation in the "value" of the work. However, under comparable worth procedures, value is measured in terms of inputs into the job (e.g., skill, effort, responsibility and working conditions) and not in terms of economic principles of the value of the output produced in the job. The exemption for differences in the bargaining power across jobs of otherwise similar value appears particularly anomalous, albeit it exists only in one jurisdiction

(Ontario) and it is allowed to apply only after pay equity has initially been achieved.

It is interesting to note that market forces are considered to be a legitimate determinant of wages when an exemption is allowed if there is an imbalance between supply and demand in the case of temporary shortages. That is, short-run wage premiums in male-dominated occupations may be allowed if demand exceeds supply for a particular male-dominated job, and the wage premiums are necessary to attract sufficient workers to reduce the shortage. No such market forces are allowed to play a role, however, if the imbalance goes in the other direction. That is, if supply exceeds demand in the female-dominated jobs that have the same job evaluation score as the male-dominated jobs, employers are not allowed to pay lower wages in the female-dominated jobs even though they can hire all the women they need at the going rate. Allowing market forces to determine wages in such situations would emasculate comparable worth policies, since prior to the comparable worth policy employers presumably were able to hire all of the women they needed at the going market wage. This highlights the fundamental difference between market forces and comparable worth as mechanisms for determining pay. Under comparable worth, employers are required to pay the same wages in female-dominated jobs as in male-dominated jobs of the same job evaluation score, even if they can hire all the women they want at the going wage in the female-dominated jobs.

In most circumstances, the allowable exemptions exist to minimize conflict with other objectives. For example, the exemptions for skill shortages, training assignments and geographic premiums exist to minimize conflict with the efficient allocation of labour resources. Exemptions for merit and seniority reduce conflict with the sacrosanct merit principle for management and the seniority principle for organized labour. Red-circling reduces conflict with principles of equity and fairness whereby workers are not required to take pay cuts if reassigned or even demoted. The exemption for differences in bargaining power at first glance appears to be a concession to unions to enable them to utilize their bargaining power to win wage gains. However, it was actually a concession to employers to prevent "leapfrogging" whereby potentially weaker female-dominated bargaining units use comparable worth to get the wage gains won by potentially stronger male-dominated bargaining units.

6.2 NO MALE COMPARATOR GROUPS AND ALL-FEMALE ESTABLISHMENTS

A difficult implementation issue arises in situations where there are no male comparator groups for making a comparison with possibly undervalued female jobs. This is especially a problem in the proactive systems whereby employers are to have a pay equity plan in place whether or not there has been a complaint or prima facie evidence of discrimination.

The issue is sometimes referred to as the "all-female establishment" issue since it obviously occurs in such situations because there are no male comparator groups within the establishment. However, the problem of no appropriate male comparators can also occur in predominantly female establishments as well as mixed establishments where there simply are no male jobs of the same job evaluation value. This can be the case, for example, if the female-dominated jobs have low job evaluation scores and the male jobs tend to have higher scores (e.g. if there is no male pay line segment above the female pay line at the low end of the job evaluation scores).

The problem of no male comparators can be particularly acute for smaller employers since there are simply few jobs for comparison purposes. Even if there is a male comparator group, if it is occupied by only one or a few incumbents, there is a greater chance that the wage may be anomalous rather than representative of the wages paid for a job of that value. The problem is compounded by the fact that such female-dominated small establishments are likely to be low paying even if they are not undervalued in the comparable worth sense. This is likely to be the case, for example, with respect to textile firms in the private sector, or day care and nursing homes in the public sector. In such circumstances, potential redress may not be available to groups who are already disadvantaged even without comparable worth initiatives.

The number of workers who are potentially excluded from coverage because male comparators are not readily available can be quite large. In the province of Ontario in Canada, a province that has gone further than anywhere else in implementing comparable worth, it is estimated that approximately one-quarter of the female workforce was potentially excluded from coverage because of the absence of male comparators with jobs of equal value (Ontario, Pay Equity Commission, 1989).

6.3   DEFINITION OF ESTABLISHMENT AND THE EMPLOYER

The definition of an establishment and the employer can have important implications for such factors as the availability of comparator groups as well as for the ability to pay for comparable worth wage adjustments. A broad definition of the organization, for example, to include different establishments in different geographic regions as long as they are under the control of a single organization, would broaden the availability of comparator groups. However, this could be at the expense of making comparisons across quite disparate work environments, especially if the parent organization grants a large degree of autonomy to its separate business units, as is increasingly the case.

Within the public sector, especially, the definition of the employer is extremely important. For a school, is it the local school board, or the Ministry of Education, or the level of government that is responsible for education budgets? For a library, is it the administrators of the particular library, or the local government department that may be responsible for the funding of the libraries? For a day-care centre, is it the day-care administrators or the government department of social services that are responsible for much of the funding? For a hospital, is it the individual hospital or the level of government that is responsible for hospital funding?

The appropriate definition of the employer depends on various factors such as the use of a common personnel and compensation policy, as well as the control of budgetary decisions that can lead to pay inequities. In practice, however, the parties have tried to have a definition established that favours their particular position. In the public sector, for example, employee groups have tried to have a broad definition established so as to expand the number of male comparator groups as well as the budgetary base for wage adjustments. As Fudge (1991, p. 66) indicates in her discussion of why nurses in Ontario were pushing to have the provincial government as employer rather than the local hospital: "Were such to be established, it would not only provide a wide range of potential comparators (the police, for example), but also result in a larger pool of money being set aside for pay equity adjustments because the government's payroll is so much larger than a hospital's."

6.4 COMPLIANCE AND ENFORCEMENT MECHANISMS

With comparable worth, as with any legislative initiative, there is the implementation issue of how best to enforce the legislation. As indicated previously, there are two main enforcement mechanisms, complaints-based and proactive.

Concern over complaints-based enforcement mechanisms have been expressed by a number of commentators who have analysed comparable worth procedures. Complaints-based systems are predicated on the assumptions that violations are the exception and not the rule, and that they are based on wilful intent and malicious conduct. These are not likely to be reasonable assumptions in the case of systemic discrimination, which can be pervasive and not necessarily based on any discriminatory intent (Kelly,1988, p. 53). Complaints-based systems may have very different impacts on the competitive position of otherwise similar firms, only a few of which are subject to a complaint, perhaps because they have a union that is knowledgeable about the issue (Robb, 1987, p. 454). The costs and complexities of litigating comparable worth have caused even those with legal training to conclude that enforcement through the courts is not likely to be a viable mechanism for comparable worth (Juriansz, 1987b, p. 670; Willborn, 1989, p. 155). Complaints-based systems have also resulted in only a small number of complaints, for many of the reasons discussed (Cihon and Wesman, 1988).

In large part because of these concerns over the complaints-based system in this particular area of anti-discrimination law, systems of proactive application have been recommended, requiring employers to institute pay equity whether or not there has been a complaint or prima facia evidence of discrimination. Since much of labour market discrimination is believed to be systemic (i.e. the pervasive but unintended by-product of other actions and personnel decisions), then solutions such as comparable worth are necessary to revamp the compensation structure, or at least that portion that gives rise to unequal pay for work of equal value. The intent is that the process would be self-managed in that once the initial obligation is established, it could be left up to the employer as to how best to achieve those requirements. This regularized requirement might then become an ingrained part of the employer's compensation system, and that this in turn would avoid costly litigation.

6.5 PHASING AND RETROACTIVITY

As with other legislative initiatives, an important design feature of comparable worth legislation is the extent to which, and the way in which, it is phased in. There are various dimensions of phasing. Comparable worth can be phased in over time and in various ways for firms of different size as well as in other sectors, especially public and private. Phasing can also exist with respect to the timing of different steps in the process.

As with other design features, there are pros and cons to the general concept of phasing. The main advantage is that phasing allows the parties time to adapt. This can be particularly important in the comparable worth area because of the complexity of the policy. At a pragmatic level, phasing also reduces the resistance to such policies. It may even reduce any negative consequences in terms of, for example, reductions in employment in response to the cost increases. Because the cost increases are phased-in, the firm may be able to adjust through less disruptive methods like attrition or reduced recruiting or other ways, rather than layoffs. The differential phasing by firm size reflects the fact that the adjustment consequences are likely to be smaller for large firms since they already tend to have job evaluation schemes and more formal compensation policies. The same is true of the public sector.

Phasing also enables the parties to learn from the mistakes made in earlier stages and to make "mid-course" corrections early. This can be important especially in system-wide proactive systems, since they are relatively new as a legislative initiative. This is also a rationale for the phasing to begin in the public sector. If mistakes are made, the costs are at least spread over the general public who pay for public sector compensation costs, usually in the form of taxes. This is likely to be more equitable than having the initial costs focused on some particular sector simply because they happen to be singled out for the initial application of the policy.

While the main advantage of phasing is that it allows the parties time to adapt, its main disadvantage is also that it allows the parties time to adapt! Firms may adjust their hiring and promotion decisions, as well as their job classification systems to alter the gender composition of their jobs so as to minimize the wage adjustments. In the extreme, investment and even plant location decisions may be made in anticipation of the subsequent adjustments. Problems of equity and fairness also arise in that otherwise similar workers who simply happen to be in an undervalued job, that is at the end of the "phasing queue", will not receive an adjustment until much later than an identical worker who happens to be in a job where pay equity is first phased in. Given the turnover that exists, especially in many of these low-paying jobs, those at the end of the phasing cycle may never receive an adjustment.

The requirement for retroactive adjustments is not likely to be a satisfactory solution in proactive systems because it does not seem reasonable to require compensation for inequities that are only uncovered through the comparable worth steps themselves. Systemic discrimination which is unintentional and the byproduct of other policies should be redressed when the problem is uncovered, and it is the uncovering of these often unintentional effects that is the purpose of the comparable worth process itself. The problem with retroactive compensation in proactive systems is compounded by the fact that employers at the end of the phasing-in stages are there usually because they will have the most difficult time adjusting (e.g. smaller employers in the private sector). Requiring large retroactive payments runs the risk that they will not survive to make the payments.

Retroactive adjustments are more appropriate in complaints-based systems when smaller numbers of employees are usually involved. The threat of having to pay such retroactive payments may be an important deterrent to prevent employers from stalling in the potentially lengthy legal proceedings that can arise. Furthermore, such complaints often arise in situations of more intentional discrimination, in which the practices are known by the employer and could be stopped at any phase in the procedure.

6.6   MAXIMUMS AND TIME-LIMITS

In proactive systems of comparable worth, ceilings or maximum amounts that must be paid are often specified, as are time-limits for making the adjustments. The ceilings are usually specified as a percentage of overall payroll, often with an annual limit and sometimes with a global ceiling that may be implied by the time period for making the adjustments (e.g. 1 per cent of overall payroll per year for four years for a total cost ceiling of 4 per cent of payroll). The ceilings are designed largely to ease the adjustment consequences for employers, and hence also the resistance to such policies.

Such cost limits are typically involved in proactive system-wide applications of comparable worth, but not in complaints-based systems. In the latter systems, smaller numbers of employees are usually involved and therefore the cost burden should not be as large as in proactive systems where one-third or more of employees can easily be involved. In complaints-based systems presumably the ability of the organization to absorb the cost is also already considered as part of the settlement. A settlement that would put the employer out of business, or even substantially jeopardize a large number of jobs, is not likely to be contemplated by any of the parties.

6.7   OBSERVATIONS ON DESIGN FEATURES

Clearly, a wide range of practical, administrative issues are involved in each and every step in the design and implementation of comparable worth. This is especially the case in the proactive systems, which are designed to lead to a fundamental restructuring of compensation systems. The design features are particularly important because they can ensure that comparable worth is properly applied, but they can also be manipulated to effectively emasculate the policy. The issue is complicated by the fact that the design features are complex and often involve technical issues that are not easily understood. There are not always right or wrong answers in this area, rather there are difficult trade-offs among a variety of legitimate competing goals and objectives.

It is unlikely that the complexity of these issues was envisaged by those who first sought to apply what seemed to be a deceptively simple principle, equal pay for work of equal value. Nevertheless, the evolution of this principle has only just begun. It is likely that more complexities will be uncovered as the application continues.

Given the complexities, and the fact that there is legitimate debate over most of these issues, it is important that the design features be discussed independently of how they may affect the outcome of a particular case. Otherwise, the stakeholders will develop positions based on how it affects their particular situation, rather than how it helps attain certain common goals. What is needed in this area is a dialogue on the common goals and how they can best be achieved through the effective design and implementation of comparable worth, as well as through other policies for achieving the same objectives.

APPLICATION IN DIFFERENT COUNTRIES

7

International comparisons are particularly difficult to make because of the different institutional and legal arrangements across countries. Furthermore, a considerable gap can exist between what is stated in the law and what is required or followed in practice. A comprehensive discussion of the legislation and practice in each country is beyond the scope of this analysis. Rather, the emphasis is on illustrating the different ways in which comparable worth can be applied in a variety of different institutional and legal environments. More detailed attention is given to Canada and the United States, since more extensive studies on comparable worth are found in these countries.

7.1   ILO CONVENTIONS AND RECOMMENDATIONS[1]

One of the ILO's most important functions is the adoption by the tripartite International Labour Conference of Conventions and Recommendations which set international labour standards. ILO member States are obliged to apply the provisions of ILO Conventions which they ratify. States are also required to report regularly on the measures taken to implement ratified Conventions.

Recommendations, which typically accompany Conventions, amplify the provisions contained in particular Conventions and provide guidelines on the manner in which those provisions may be implemented in practice. Recommendations are not open to ratification.

The ILO has an elaborate supervisory procedure to assess and promote the application of ratified Conventions, undertaken initially by a Committee of Experts which determines compliance on the basis of an independent, impartial and objective evaluation. Further supervision is undertaken by tripartite bodies of the ILO.

The Equal Remuneration Convention (No. 100), adopted in 1951, sets out the principle of equal pay for work of equal value. The Convention focuses only on wage discrimination between men and women. Article 1 of Convention No. 100 defines remuneration broadly to cover all payments in cash or in kind, including any employment-related benefits, allowances, bonuses or other advantages. Article 2 requires the principle of equal pay to cover all workers, and to be applied by any combination of national laws or regulations, legally established or recognized machinery for wage determination, or collective agreements. While job evaluation is not specifically required, Article 3 of the Convention states that an objective appraisal of jobs shall be performed where such action will assist in ensuring and promoting equal pay for work of equal value. Convention No. 100 has been ratified by over 110 countries.

The Equal Remuneration Recommendation, 1951 (No. 90), which was adopted to supplement Convention No. 100, states that governments should take appropriate action after consultation with workers' organizations to:

(1) ensure the application of equal remuneration for all employees of centralized government departments or agencies, or for employees subject to such statutory regulation or public control (e.g. through minimum wages, public ownership or public contracts);

(2) encourage its application to employees of state, provincial or local government departments or agencies, where these have jurisdiction over remuneration;

(3) provide for the legal enactment of the general application of the principle of equal remuneration for work of equal value.

In addition to the Equal Remuneration Convention and Recommendation of 1951, which refer to discrimination in pay, the ILO also has the Discrimination (Employment and Occupation) Convention (No. 111), and Recommendation (No. 111). These were both adopted in 1958, to come into force in 1960. They have been ratified by more than 100 countries, usually but not always the same countries that have ratified the equal pay convention and recommendation.

Convention No. 111 and Recommendation No. 111 prohibit discrimination on grounds of race, colour, sex, religion, political opinion, national extraction or social origin in regard to access to vocational training, access to employment and to particular occupations and terms and conditions of employment. Not all distinctions, exclusions or preferences are deemed to be discriminatory within the meaning of the Convention. Differentiation between candidates for a particular job which is based on objective and necessary requirements to carry out the work does not constitute discrimination under the terms of the Convention. Special measures for protection or assistance afforded to the target groups are also explicitly permitted under the instruments. Recommendation No. 111 states that all persons should, without discrimination, enjoy equality of opportunity and treatment in respect of remuneration of work of equal value, thereby also including comparable worth within the framework of measures to be taken to combat employment discrimination in general. Since Recommendation No. 111 deals with discrimination in areas such as race, colour, religion, political opinion, national extraction or social origin as well as sex, in theory this means that comparable worth could be applied to these groups as well as to females. Furthermore, Recommendation No. 111 does not limit the obligation only to the public sector. In theory, therefore, Convention No. 111 and Recommendation No. 111 could be interpreted as a broad requirement for comparable worth to be applied to a number of groups and across all sectors. In practice, however, comparable worth issues are dealt with as part of Convention No. 90 and Recommendation No. 100, with its focus on women and its initial application to the public sector in signatory countries.

EC Legislation

The principle of comparable worth was also incorporated into European Community (EC) law.[2] Article 119 of the original Treaty of Rome of 1957 required equal pay for *equal work*. There was considerable uncertainty as to whether this required equal pay for work of *equal value*. This uncertainty was removed by the Equal Pay Directive of 1975, which indicated that the principle of equal pay was to apply to work of equal value as well as to the same work. As with Convention No. 100, all aspects of remuneration were to be considered in the definition of pay, the focus was on sex discrimination alone, and job evaluation procedures were sanctioned but not required for determining the value of jobs. Although instruments such as the Equal Pay Directive are binding, it is left up to the Member States as to how to implement the Directive. The EC legislation also takes precedence over national laws and is directly enforceable.

Compliance in the member countries was fostered by three main mechanisms: infringement proceedings; preliminary rulings made by the European Court of Justice; and staff actions of the Court of Justice. Infringement proceedings were brought by the Commission of the EC against seven Member States, Belgium, Denmark, France, the Federal Republic of Germany, Luxembourg, the Netherlands and the United Kingdom. The proceedings basically required the laws in the Member States to be amended in conformity with the EC law.

In addition, the EC Directive has been extended to Member States through preliminary rulings made by the Court of Justice in response to requests from the courts and tribunals of Member States. The requests were made in order to establish precedents to deal with the individual litigation that was now possible under EC law. The Court of Justice itself has also instituted a number of staff actions in its capacity as an administrative tribunal where its own staff can bring forth a complaint. Preliminary rulings and decisions on staff action cases have been made on a variety of matters: pay is to be broadly defined to include contributions to a retirement scheme and benefits in kind; comparisons can be made with males who *previously* occupied the job; hourly pay differences can exist between part-time and full-time jobs, but only if based on objective factors other than sex; physical strength can be a legitimate job criterion; equal pay cannot be attained by reducing the pay of overpaid men; and comparisons can be made even if the job of the claimant is of higher value.

There appears to be some uncertainty in the EC as to whether comparable worth comparisons can be made across different establishments or organizations. In Canada and the United States such comparisons across different organizations are not allowed, although there can be debate over the definition of the employer, and many of the applications have been across all units of a state or provincial government. In the EC countries there appears to be agreement that comparisons should be based on concrete appraisals of the work actually performed by employees of different sexes within the same establishment. However, comparisons can be made across the different job sites of the same employer. Dutch legislation also explicitly allowed comparisons across different establishments if internal comparisons were not available (although that provision was dropped in subsequent amendments). What has not yet been clarified, is the definition of the employer in the case of the public sector, or in the case of mergers, alliances and joint ventures in the private sector.

Although individual litigation is possible under EC legislation, it tends to be relatively uncommon in member countries, with the possible exception of the United Kingdom.[3] This dearth of litigation in the EC most likely reflects a variety of factors. The European legal tradition tends to recognize only individual litigation and not "class action" suits or group complaints. Comparable worth comparisons, however, are particularly ill-suited to individual complaints, given the cost and complexities of challenging job evaluation procedures and collective agreements. The issue is further complicated by the fact that the use of analytical job evaluation schemes for the specific purpose of applying comparable worth is not common in most EC countries (except for the Netherlands, Germany and the United Kingdom). While the burden of proof tends to fall on individual complainants rather than on defendant employers in most EC countries, this situation is changing in light of the 1988 proposal for an EC Council Directive on reversing the burden of proof in the area of equal pay and equal treatment for women and men. Individual complainants are also deterred by the costs and by the fear of reprisals. Enforcement agencies in Europe tend not to act on behalf of, or assist individual litigants in their cases, although there are exceptions.[4]

In many European countries, centralized collective agreements, usually negotiated at the level of the industry and region, provide a potentially important mechanism for the implementation of pay equity. This remains true in spite of the trend towards decentralization at the plant level as centralized collective bargaining is still very active for wage-fixing purposes.

These agreements have incorporated the *principle* of comparable worth, but whether they have implemented it in *practice* remains an unanswered question. In Germany, for example, pressure to implement it in practice is weakened by the fact that the legislation does not provide for any independent agency to administer the law and ensure compliance. Such functions are to be conducted by the works councils of each enterprise, consisting of employer and employee representatives.

In Sweden[5] egalitarian wage policies, including equal pay for work of equal value, are principles that tend to be adhered to for all workers as part of the centralized collective bargaining that exists over the "social wage".

7.2 CANADA[6]

Canada's experience of comparable worth (termed pay equity in that country) is informative because it has the most extensive application of the principle. Furthermore, the various jurisdictions incorporate different forms of the legislation, therefore providing variability in the procedures.

Canada is a federal country with jurisdiction over labour issues in the hands of 13 jurisdictions: ten provinces, two territories and the federal jurisdiction, the latter covering approximately 10 per cent of the workforce. All jurisdictions in Canada have some form of comparable worth legislation or regulation, except for the provinces of Alberta and Saskatchewan. The legislation was generally adopted in the late 1970s and throughout the 1980s. Five jurisdictions (Manitoba, Ontario, Prince Edward Island, Nova Scotia, and New Brunswick) have proactive legislation, which puts the onus on the employer to implement pay equity, whether or not there has been a complaint. Newfoundland and British Columbia require a proactive procedure, but through the collective bargaining procedure with their public employees, rather than through legislation.

In general, those jurisdictions that have proactive legislation limit its application to the public sector, broadly defined to include municipalities, hospitals, schools, universities and crown corporations, as well as to government employees. In practice, the complaints-based systems have also been applied almost exclusively to the public sector.

The exception to this limitation to the public sector is Ontario where the legislation has been phased into the private sector, beginning first with large companies. In that vein, the jurisdiction of Ontario is at the leading edge in Canada, indeed in the world, in that it has both proactive legislation and applies that legislation to the private as well as the public sector. For that reason, the emerging experience of Ontario merits careful attention and analysis.

Gender dominance of a job class is defined in different ways: 70 per cent more of either sex (Federal jurisdiction and Manitoba); 60 per cent female and 70 per cent male (Ontario, New Brunswick); and 60 per cent or more of either sex (Prince Edward Island and Nova Scotia). The federal jurisdiction also uses a sliding scale for the male jobs, using 70 per cent for smaller establishments of under 100 employees, 60 per cent for mid-size establishments of 100 to 500 employees, and 55 per cent for large establishments of over 500 employees.

The use of wage lines relating pay to job evaluation points are specifically mentioned in the legislation of three jurisdictions, while job-to-job comparisons are specifically required in two jurisdictions. Ceilings or limits on the costs (typically 1 per cent of payroll) or time periods for the attainment of pay equity (usually four or five years) are often specified. The number and type of allowable exemptions range from zero to seven.

Canada does not have extensive experience with litigation in the anti-discrimination area, although more is emerging in the proactive system in Ontario.[7] Rather than litigation through the courts, the emphasis has been on enforcement through administrative agencies and tribunals responsible for enforcing employment standards or human rights and anti-discrimination legislation. In such agencies, the emphasis tends to be on conciliation and negotiated solutions as well as on educating the parties as to their responsibilities. The decisions of such agencies are subject to judicial review; however, the courts have generally been loath to intervene in those decisions.

7.3 UNITED STATES[8]

While Canada may have progressed further than any other country with the implementation of comparable worth, the application of the procedure to substantial numbers of employees first began in the United States. The analysis of the concept, and its implementation especially through job evaluation, has been most developed in that country.

Federal legislation and court interpretations

In the United States, federal legislation generally takes precedence over state legislation, although the latter can enhance the federal law by providing more extensive protection or coverage. This has turned out to be important in the comparable worth area because the federal law has generally not been sympathetic to the notion of comparable worth, while it has been advanced by a number of state laws. In the federal area, the two main legislative initiatives dealing with equal pay are the Equal Pay Act of 1963 and Title VII of the Civil Rights Act of 1964.

The Equal Pay Act of 1963 required equal pay for "equal work in jobs the performance of which requires equal skill, effort and responsibility, and which are performed under similar working conditions". Although these are the factors upon which equal value comparisons are made, Congress explicitly rejected the notion of comparable worth by changing the phraseology of the original proposal, which involved the phrase "for work of comparable character in jobs the performance of which requires comparable skills", to the more narrow concept of equal work (Weiler, 1986). Title VII, the Equal Employment Opportunity (EEO) Amendment of the Civil Rights Act of 1964, prohibits both wage and employment opportunity discrimination, and it prohibits them on the basis of factors such as race, colour, religion and national origin, as well as sex.

Title VII was to be administered by the EEO Commission. Initially there was some uncertainty as to whether Title VII restricted comparisons to "equal work", as is clearly the case under the Equal Pay Act, or whether it would encompass the broader concept of comparable worth.

Subsequent court interpretations have generally rejected the concept of comparable worth. In 1985 the United States Court of Appeal reversed an earlier decision involving the American Federation of State, County and Municipal Employees (AFSCME) v. the State of Washington. The appeal court decision explicitly stated that the law was not intended to "abrogate fundamental economic principles such as the laws of supply and demand or to prevent employers from competing in the labour market". The appeal court also rejected the notion that the concept of "disparate impact" could be applied to wage determination as opposed to employment practices like height and weight requirements. It also rejected the notions that job evaluation results were sufficient to establish discrimination, and that employers should be bound by the results of their own job evaluation studies.

This rejection of comparable worth and acceptance of market principles for determining the "worth" of a job have been advanced in numerous other American court cases. In *Christensen v. State of Iowa* (1977), the court indicated: "Appellant's theory ignores economic realities. The value of the job to the employer represents but one factor affecting wages. Other factors may include the supply of workers willing to do the job and the ability of the workers to band together to bargain collectively for higher wages."

In *Lemons v. City and County of Denver* (1980), the court indicated that the law does not require an employer "to ignore the market in setting wages for genuinely different work classifications and that differing rates for differing occupations could be justified by reference to market rates". In *American Nurses' Association v. Illinois* (1986), the court indicated that: "The issue of comparable worth is not the sort that judges are well equipped to resolve intelligently ... and that such a legal requirement should not be read into either Title VII or the Constitution ... Because jobs do not have an intrinsic value that can be scientifically measured, the limitations inherent in job evaluation techniques prohibit the proposed extension of Title VII."

These court decisions illustrate the rejection of the concept of comparable worth by the American judiciary. As stated by Willborn (1989, p. 10) in commenting on the appeals decision for the state of Washington: "As a strict legal matter the final result, the court of appeals decision, would stand for the proposition that comparable worth cases could not be won in the United States." Clearly, use of the mechanism of litigation through the courts in the United States will have to await a judiciary and an administration that is less hostile to regulation and interference with market forces.

State and local legislation and activity for the public sector

While the avenue of litigation through the courts for comparable worth has been largely closed off in the United States, at least for the time being, numerous state and local governments have undertaken comparable worth activity in various ways (National Committee on Pay Equity (1989)):

(1) **research or data collection** – monitoring pay equity in other states, holding public hearings, studying the issue in general; identifying the wage gap and occupational segregation (44 states);

(2) **pay equity study** – quantitative or point-factor system to evaluate dissimilar jobs and compare salaries in female- and male-dominated jobs or minority job categories (23 states);

(3) **pay equity adjustment** – actual adjustments have been made or appropriated, often in response to lawsuits for single classifications and sometimes in response to widespread implementation at the state level (20 states).

(4) **pay equity implementation** – broad-based proactive implementation to a large number of public sector employees, based on systematic job evaluation and a pay equity plan (the six states of Minnesota, Iowa, Oregon, Washington, New York and Wisconsin). Minnesota is the only state, however, that has legislated the requirement as opposed to approved a budget and then subsequently implemented pay equity (Weiler, 1991, p. 343). Washington State enacted legislation in 1983 requiring comparable worth for all state employees by 1993. However, this legislation involved paying all employees according to a single pay line, and not specifically raising the pay in female-dominated jobs to the pay of male-dominated jobs (Government Accounting Office, 1992). At the local level, there has also been comparable worth activity in such forms as undertaking a study, undergoing litigation, passing a local ordinance, or contemplating or implementing comparable worth. Such activity has occurred in cities, municipalities, counties, school districts and colleges and universities. It has been particularly prominent in states like California, Minnesota and Washington.

State legislation for the private sector

Since the late 1980s, 15 of the state anti-discrimination laws have required private sector employers to pay men and women equally for comparable work (Willborn 1986). While this gives the appearance of considerable private sector activity in the comparable worth area, once again legislative appearances can be quite different from what exists in practice. More specifically, no comparable worth cases have been litigated under the state laws. This most likely reflects the fact that many of the state laws were enacted in an earlier period and were not intended to mean comparable worth in the sense used today, that is, involving job evaluations with comparisons across dissimilar occupations. Their intent was more to allow comparisons of comparable *work* (i.e. substantially similar work), not comparable *worth* (i.e. equal pay for work of equal value) (Cook, 1985, p. 4). In essence, comparable worth, where it exists in the United States, is largely a public sector phenomenon. Of course this does not preclude that it may be a voluntary private sector practice, although such procedures are likely to be rare.

7.4 AUSTRALIA[9]

Australia is often singled out in the comparable worth area because of its unusual system whereby wages are determined for most workers by a system of wage tribunals. Prior to 1950, the basic wage for women was set at 54 per cent of the wages of men in the same job. The rationale was that women did not need to support a family. Around 1950, this "official markdown" was changed to 75 per cent of male wages.

This institutionalized wage discrimination was eliminated in two ways. The first involved eliminating the markdown for women who worked in the same jobs as men. This was done in 1969, to be fully implemented by 1972. It was termed equal pay because women were to receive the same pay as men if they did the same job. Female-dominated jobs, however, were exempt from this procedure but were later also covered in 1972, with implementation by 1975. This was termed comparable worth because it involved eliminating official discrimination against the female-dominated jobs.

This is not comparable worth, however, in the usual sense of eliminating wage differentials between jobs of equal value within the same organization, where value is determined by a procedure such as job evaluation. Rather, it is a procedure of centralized wage fixing, and one where systematic wage discrimination that was established by decree was removed by subsequent decree. Since the 1972 comparable worth awards by the wage-setting tribunals, there has been little activity in this area, in part because of concern over the potential cost implications. As indicated by Killingsworth (1990, p. 238) and Kramar and Plowman (1991, p. 69) a number of recent tribunal decisions specifically rejected the concept of comparable worth, at least as it tends to be practised in the United States, Canada and the United Kingdom. In fact, the comparable worth principle has been criticized for involving comparisons across jobs that are not related or similar. Such a critique, of course, gets to the very heart of comparable worth since it is specifically designed to make comparisons across otherwise unrelated or dissimilar jobs, provided they are deemed to be of equal value according to some job evaluation procedure.

Recent activities in this area in Australia have been confined to a small number of complaints to the tribunals, usually on the part of predominantly female health-care professionals, for reclassification into the same categories of other male-dominated professions, so as to receive the higher pay. The settlements are not really comparable worth settlements in the sense of utilizing job evaluations and adjusting wages to the pay of male jobs of the same score. As stated by Rafferty (1991, p. 5) in commenting on one case in 1988: "The salary adjustment, which was an agreed component of the resolution, was not based on a factor by factor evaluation of the work of dental therapists but was arrived at by agreement through a process of negotiation closely akin to horse-trading, as a means of avoiding an arbitrated decision."

There has also been a shift in wage-fixing arrangements towards a much greater focus on workplace bargaining. The Australian Industrial Relations Commission has established a new enterprise-bargaining principle which allows for wage rises to be negotiated between unions and employers in return for productivity changes at the workplace level. These arrangements are underpinned by an enforceable award framework with classifications established on a comparative work value basis, which is being undertaken as part of a review of award wage relativities (a process called the minimum rates adjustment (MRA) process). The aim of the MRA process is to ensure that work performed under individual award classifications is valued appropriately in comparison with benchmark classifications and with classifications within the same award – on the basis of skill, responsibility, and the conditions under which the work is normally performed. In this way, equal value principles are being incorporated more generally into the Australian system of wage setting.

7.5 CONCLUDING OBSERVATIONS

The previous discussion highlights the vast differences that can exist across countries in the application of comparable worth. While generalizations on international comparisons are hazardous, a number of observations can be made.

– The vast differences in the legal and institutional arrangements that exist across countries in their wage-determination mechanisms suggest that no one single best approach to comparable worth is likely to prevail. Rather than a "one-size-fits-all" approach, different procedures are likely to be necessary, tailored to the particular wage-setting arrangements of the different countries.

– Individual complaints-based procedures do not seem to lead to much activity in the comparable worth area. This may be so because of the usual cost and delays and because the burden of proof usually falls on the complainant, an especially onerous requirement in this area given the complexities involved in the procedure. Allowing unions to instigate the complaint or assist individuals can help in this regard, but unions also come up against obstacles. In most countries that allow enforcement agencies to lodge a complaint, this procedure seldom gets applied, especially if the agency also deals with other labour issues. Similarly, labour inspectors, even if they are allowed to instigate a complaint based on their regular inspection process, seldom do so, in part because they have other areas of concern, they are often understaffed, and they may not have the expertise required in this complex area.

– Centralized wage-determination procedures provide a viable mechanism for increasing the wages of females relative to males However, this is not comparable worth in the conventional sense with its various implementation steps within the establishment. Rather it involves a variety of possible procedures: an overall egalitarian wage policy (e.g. as in Sweden); elimination of official "markdowns" in female-dominated jobs as in the wage decrees through tribunals (e.g. Australia); elimination of separate male and female minimum wages in collective agreements or wage awards (e.g. Australia). Such systems facilitate raising the wages of women because market forces are already blunted, and institutional mechanisms exist to change wages, often by simply eliminating official separate rates.

– Proactive policies of comparable worth can also ensure that the policy is implemented as an integral part of the employer's overall compensation system since it is required whether or not a complaint has been made. However, our experience with such procedures is still limited to a few jurisdictions in Canada and the United States that have adopted such a policy, usually only for their public sector employees. The emerging experience of the province of Ontario in Canada merits careful observation because it has legislated a proactive requirement on employers in the private sector as well as in the public sector.

– Such proactive systems have their problems, however, not the least of which are the technical and legal issues associated with each stage of implementation.

– There are vast differences between having a law "on the books" and having it applied in practice. Having the legislation itself is no guarantee that it will be effectively applied, and in fact may be a "smokescreen" for doing nothing. Conversely, considerable action can occur without specific legislation. Obviously having a good law effectively applied is the best alternative, but legislation is neither a necessary nor sufficient condition for the effective implementation of comparable worth.

– Continued monitoring and evaluation of the different experiences across countries in this area is absolutely essential. This will add to our understanding of the pros and cons of the different alternatives, as well as facilitate the emergence of "best practices" in this important area.

Notes

[1] Information on the ILO Conventions and Recommendations, and on the European Community Law discussed in the next section, is contained in Bellace (1980), Goodwin (1984), ILO (1986), Landau (1984), McCrudden (1987, 1991), von Prondzynski (1988), Shamie (1986), Schmid and Weitzel (1984), Weiner and Gunderson (1990) and Willborn (1986a, 1991).

[2] The Treaty of Rome which governs the European Community (EC), formerly the European Community (EEC) also incorporates the principle of comparable worth. The EC consists of 12 nations. The six founding members, Belgium, France, Italy, Luxembourg, the Netherlands and the Federal Republic of Germany established the EEC in 1957. They were joined by Denmark, Ireland, and the United Kingdom in 1973, Greece in 1981, and Portugal and Spain in 1986.

[3] In the United Kingdom, the individual female complainant selects the male within the establishment to whom she feels her work is comparable. The Equal Employment Opportunity Commission first tries to handle the complaint by conciliation. If that fails, then an outside expert writes a report, based on explicit or implicit job evaluation, and a tribunal makes a subsequent judgement.

[4] The current French legislation allows unions and labour inspectors as well as individual workers to bring forth complaints. Conciliation is attempted, and if that is unsuccessful the matter goes to an industrial tribunal with ultimate appeal to a higher court. Once the complaint is made, the burden of proof falls on the employer.

[5] The role of women, and of anti-discrimination law, in the Swedish labour market is discussed in the articles by Lofstrom and Gustafson and by Victorin in Willborn (1991).

[6] The Canadian experience is described, for example, in Chaykowski (1990), Cihon and Wesman (1988), Gunderson (1989b), Gunderson and Riddell (1992), Gunderson and Robb (1991a, 1991b), Juriansz (1987a 1987b), Kelly (1988), McDermott (1990), and Robb (1987).

[7] Jurisprudence in this area in Canada is discussed in Gunderson and Robb (1991b) and Juriansz (1987a).

[8] The experience with comparable worth is discussed in many of the American studies referred to in the bibliography. Particular references include Aldrich and Buchele (1986), Bellace (1984), Blumrosen (1986), Cook (1985), Goodwin (1984), Weiler (1986), and Willborn (1986a, 1989).

[9] The Australian experience is discussed in Bennett (1988), Burton et al. (1987), Gregory and Duncan (1981), Gregory, Anstie, Daly and Ho (1989), Gregory and Daly (1991), Killingsworth (1990), Kramar and Plowman (1991), Rafferty (1989, 1991) and Shortt (1986).

THEORETICALLY EXPECTED IMPACT
OF COMPARABLE WORTH

8

8.1 EXPECTED WAGE AND NON-WAGE EFFECTS ON COVERED WORKERS

Comparable worth should obviously increase the wages of covered employees in otherwise undervalued female-dominated jobs. The extent to which firms will raise wages in undervalued female jobs depends upon the extent to which they can pass the cost increase to customers in the private sector, and to taxpayers in the public sector. In private sector markets that are extremely competitive, it may be difficult to pass these cost increases forward to customers. This is especially the case with countries under increasing global competition that may not have, or may not enforce, comparable worth legislation, let alone other basic labour laws. Given the increasing mobility of capital and the ability of employers to shift production to countries that offer a "hospitable" business climate, countries may be reluctant to overly regulate employers for fear that they will not attract or retain business.

This greater corporate mobility and flexibility of plant location decisions, means that corporations may also flee tax increases as well as overly restrictive labour and other regulations.

In public sector markets it is also becoming increasingly difficult to pass cost increases to taxpayers. Public sector retrenchment and scrutiny is becoming increasingly common, as resistance to increases in taxes or deficits grows.

In addition to passing legislated wage cost increases "forward" to customers and taxpayers, firms are likely to try to pass some of the cost increases "backward" to their workforce, including the groups who may be receiving the legislated wage increases. For those groups, employers may try to offset some of the cost increase by changing other non-wage aspects of employment, such as the pace of work or fringe benefits. These adjustments may be limited, however, by the fact that such changes should be incorporated into the skill, effort, responsibility or working conditions of subsequent job evaluations, thereby raising the "value" of the job and hence the required pay. Moreover, many fringe benefits are wage related so that comparable worth wage increases lead to greater fringe benefits. This is the case, for example, with (earnings based) pensions, vacation pay, sick leave pay and life insurance policies.

8.2   EXPECTED WAGE EFFECTS ON NON-COVERED WORKERS

Firms may also try to shift some of the cost increases "backward" to employees in male-dominated jobs that are "overvalued" according to the job evaluation procedure. There are a number of ways of identifying the overvalued male jobs in such a procedure. The legislation usually prohibits the overt lowering of wages in a male comparator job, but it cannot prevent slower rates of wage increases going to the overvalued male-dominated jobs.

In situations of collective bargaining, especially, there may be concern that the funds for comparable worth adjustments will come out of the general pool of funds available for wage increases. The same concern is applicable to elements of the public sector when budgets are allocated by the government. It is for these reasons that unions and workers usually want comparable worth adjustments to be negotiated and awarded separately from bargaining over the new collective agreement. Moreover, they usually want comparable worth adjustments to be separate items in the public sector budget determination process, and not part of the more general determination of the labour budget.

Comparable worth legislation may also affect the wages of non-covered workers indirectly through the basic market forces of supply and demand. To the extent that there is any adverse employment effect from the wages being set above the market determined wage (discussed subsequently), then any workers displaced from the covered sector will augment the supply of labour in the non-covered sector and thereby lower wages. The demand for non-covered workers may increase to the extent that they are used as a substitute for the more expensive covered workers. The demand for non-covered workers, however, may decrease to the extent that they are complementary to the covered workers, or the cost increases lead to a reduction in output and hence the derived demand for both covered and non-covered workers.

Institutional forces can also be at work. The wages of non-covered workers may fall (i.e. realistically, they only rise more slowly) since there are less "funds" to go around, unless of course the legislation attracts an infusion of funds, as may occur in the public sector. The wages of non-covered workers may also fall if the job evaluation procedure reveals them to be "overvalued". In contrast, the wages of non-covered workers may rise if there is pressure to restore at least some of the old wage relativities.

Firms may try to offset the cost of comparable worth wage adjustments by becoming more efficient in other areas, the so-called "shock effect" whereby the legislated cost increase shocks management into other more efficient practices. Wage cost increases also may be offset, in part at least, by positive effects on the behaviour of the recipients of the wage adjustment, such as reduced turnover and improved morale and commitment.

8.3 EXPECTED EMPLOYMENT AND LONGER RUN EFFECTS

To the extent that firms are not able to pass the cost increases forward to customers or taxpayers, or backward to workers, or to absorb them through shock effects or reductions in profits, then the wage cost increases can lead to reductions in the employment opportunities for the female-dominated jobs receiving the legislated wage increase. This occurs as employers substitute other inputs (including non-covered employees) for the now more expensive covered workers. In addition, the higher cost and hence prices reduce the demand for the output of the firm and hence their derived demand for all inputs including covered and non-covered employees.

Kahn (1992) discussed other theoretical possibilities whereby wage increases engendered by comparable worth may not lead to reductions in the employment opportunities of women. If public sector employers are the dominant employer in a local labour market, they may be wage setters (i.e. monopsonists) and not wage takers, in which case they may not reduce employment in response to wage increases. Furthermore, in union bargaining models, unions may be able to bargain for higher wages and employment, largely at the expense of employer profits. In the comparable worth context, it is also possible that an increase in the pay of female-dominated jobs could increase the proportion of women in those jobs, especially if accompanied by other initiatives like affirmative action. This could counter any tendency for more males to enter those occupations in response to the higher pay.

Comparable worth legislation may affect wages and employment in a variety of more subtle ways. For example, if higher wages are paid in the female-dominated jobs, then this may discourage occupational mobility out of those jobs and into the otherwise better paying male-dominated and mixed jobs. As with any wage-fixing legislation, comparable worth may discourage women from accepting low wages in return for training or other human capital investments that could improve long-term wage growth.

In the longer run, many of the adjustments that were previously discussed as giving rise to an adverse employment effect in response to the legislated wage increase will have sufficient time to occur. This can be the case, for example, with respect to such adjustments as subcontracting, reduced new hiring, and investment and plant location decisions. The extent to which these will occur, of course, depends upon the magnitude of the cost increase associated with the comparable worth adjustment.

Clearly, comparable worth legislation can have a variety of impacts. It should increase the wages of covered workers, although it can have an ambiguous effect on the wages of non-covered workers. Employment will likely grow more slowly in jobs that experience large legislated wage increases. Since many of these effects work in opposing directions, and since theory does not shed light on the magnitude of these effects, it is necessary to appeal to the empirical evidence to determine the net effect of comparable worth and the magnitude of that effect.

EVIDENCE FROM NORTH AMERICAN CASES

9

This chapter presents the empirical evidence on the magnitude of the settlements and the effects of comparable worth in specific cases where the policy has been applied. The next chapter deals with the evidence on other broader dimensions: econometric studies on the impact on the overall male-female wage gap in the economy as a whole; econometric studies of the employment impact; and studies that deal with other dimensions such as the effect on wage structures and attitudes of the parties.

The specific cases where comparable worth has been applied tend to provide information on such factors as: the magnitude of the wage adjustment that has occurred; the proportion of the workforce in those particular cases who receive the adjustment; the extent to which the adjustment reduces the overall male-female wage gap in the organization; and the overall cost to the firm, usually expressed as a percentage increase in payroll cost. The cases reviewed in this chapter are North American, since that is where such impact studies have been conducted.[1] As such, they are most relevant for providing information on applications that have similar characteristics to those outlined in the specific cases.

9.1 WASHINGTON STATE: THE EARLIEST EXPERIENCE

Washington State[2] was the innovator in the comparable worth procedure, with the government commissioning a comparable worth study in 1974. Pay lines were estimated in male-dominated and female-dominated jobs, with the pay in the female jobs being about 20 per cent below the pay in the male jobs of the same job evaluation scores.

The government refused to implement any adjustments in response to the study, and after losing a lower court decision in 1983, it won its case on appeals in 1985. Rather than undergoing further appeals to the Supreme Court, the government and the main union (the American Federation of State, County and Municipal Employees, AFSCME) agreed to an out-of-court settlement. A small adjustment was made in 1984, with the major adjustments being phased in from 1986 to 1992. A corridor approach was used, with female-dominated jobs that were more than 15 per cent below the male pay line initially being brought up to 15 per cent below the male line. Female jobs that were below the male pay line but within the 15 per cent corridor, were awarded a 2.5 per cent increase.

At the same time that those comparable worth adjustments were occurring, the state also passed legislation requiring "comparable worth" for all state employees (not just those in female-dominated jobs). This took the form of requiring pay to be based on an overall pay line for all employees (U.S. General Accounting Office, 1992).

Over the period 1983 to 1987, when implementation of comparable worth began, the ratio of female-to-male earnings increased from 0.802 to 0.856, an increase of 0.054 (i.e. 0.856-0.802) which was 27 per cent of the original gap of 0.198 (i.e. 1-0.802). This increase in the ratio of female-to-male earnings was about twice the increase that occurred in the economy as a whole, highlighting that forces other than comparable worth were also at work reducing the gap.

9.2   MINNESOTA STATE EMPLOYEES: TEXTBOOK APPLICATION [3]

As stated by Evans and Nelson (1989, p. 3): "The implementation of comparable worth for its state and local employees has proceeded further in Minnesota than in any other state in the nation." They indicate that the application has been smooth because of a number of key ingredients. A well-developed job evaluation system was already in place, and the comparable worth wage adjustment process could be grafted onto that system without endless technocratic debate and litigation over the process. The legislation gave a clear legal obligation and mandate to the parties in that comparable worth was to be *the* principal policy for wage setting for state employees. The adversarial procedure that was present in the debate over the legislation itself was not carried over into the implementation phase, as women's groups that were so crucial to getting the law passed were not involved in its subsequent implementation which was an internal government process. The union and management representatives were very capable and in mutual agreement over the importance of the policy; this also facilitated advance agreement over many of the implementation procedures. The comparable worth implementation was carried out separately from the normal collective bargaining and salary determination process, so as to minimize any adversarial spillovers from collective bargaining and so as to minimize the appearance that there might be redistribution from some groups to others.

Under the State Employees Pay Equity Act of 1984, state government employees received comparable worth wage adjustments in each of the years 1985, 1986 and 1987. The adjustments averaged US$2,200 per recipient at an overall cost of 3.7 per cent of payroll. The ratio of female-to-male earnings was 0.74 prior to the comparable worth adjustment, and 0.82 after the adjustment, so that the adjustment closed 31 per cent (i.e. 0.08/0.26) of the gap. The remaining 69 per cent of the gap was not closed because it reflected two factors: differences in the skill, effort, responsibility and working conditions between male- and female-dominated jobs; and the fact that many women were not eligible for wage adjustments because they did not work in female-dominated jobs.

Killingsworth (1990) calculated the wage effects of comparable worth by estimating a regression equation with the conventional determinants of earnings as explanatory variables. Dummy variables were then included to capture whether comparable worth applied for the particular individual or job. He estimated the cumulative wage gains attributable to comparable worth over the three-year implementation period to be 11.7 percentage points for females and 1.8 percentage points for males. These cumulative effects thereby raised the ratio of female-to-male earnings by 9.9 percentage points. Males received comparable worth adjustments because about 10 per cent of the beneficiaries were men who were in undervalued female-dominated jobs.

9.3 MINNESOTA LOCAL GOVERNMENT EMPLOYEES: A CONTRASTING EXPERIENCE

Following the apparent success of comparable worth for state government employees, the legislation was extended to local government employees through the Local Government Pay Equity Act of 1984. In sharp contrast to the implementation for state employees, however, implementation at the local level did not work smoothly.

All of the ingredients for successful implementation under the legislation for state government employees appear to have been absent for local government employees. Well-developed job evaluation systems were not already in place, and therefore the choice of the appropriate system became the subject of intense technocratic debate. Obviously, at local levels it is difficult to expect the parties to always have expertise in these issues. The legislation itself did not give a clear legal obligation and mandate to the parties in that it stated that comparable worth was to be a primary consideration for wage setting for state employees (not necessarily *the* primary consideration as indicated in the state law). Moreover, the local legislation did not involve any appropriation of funds to pay for the adjustment, the legislation was imposed from above with the local governments left on their own to find the funds.

Local governments were not always unionized and, where they were, the job evaluation and other implementation decisions were often in the hands of local managers. Technical expertise was often absent, and mistrust was common. Local managers did not usually fully appreciate the importance of the policy and resisted its implementation as being imposed from "above". Since they largely controlled the implementation process, they also had the technocratic means to manage the change, which usually meant minimizing the change. When change occurred it often became a restructuring of the whole compensation process so that other groups also gained at the expense of a lack of focus on female-dominated jobs. The comparable worth implementation procedure often became part of the normal salary-determination process, so the redistributive nature of the process was highlighted as gains to some groups often came at the direct expense of losses to others. Cost-containment measures affecting other specific groups were often put in place. If other groups had the political power, however, they could utilize the process to improve their own position.

Systematic evidence on the effects of comparable worth for local government employees is not available. However, Evans and Nelson (1989, pp. 128-133, 160) indicate that preliminary evidence suggests direct cost increases of around 2 to 4 per cent of payroll, averaging 2.6 per cent. There is wide variation, however, ranging from 0 to 10 per cent. These are likely to be lower bounds, since they reflect the wage adjustments only for persons in female-dominated jobs. Because other groups were often involved in the process, their pay was also often adjusted upwards to restore some internal equity.

9.4   IOWA: INTEREST GROUPS AND THE AMENDMENT PROCESS

In the state of Iowa, additional cost increases were also imposed as other groups became involved in the process to protect or further their own interests (Orazem and Mattila, 1990). Specifically, when the comparable worth steps were originally applied, they would have increased the overall ratio of female-to-male earnings from 0.78 to 0.88, thereby closing 44 per cent of the overall gap. However, this would have led to pay cuts for professionals and union members. These groups were able to bring pressure to amend the plan so that their potential losses were converted to gains, which came at the expense of reduced gains for women, as well as an additional infusion of public funds to pay for the amendments. In the end, the wages of both men and women increased as a result of the process. Specifically, the wages of men increased by 6.0 per cent and the wages of women increased by 12.3 per cent, with the larger increase for women leading to an increase in the ratio of female-to-male earnings from 0.78 to 0.83, thereby closing 22 per cent of the overall gap. In other words, the amendments led to a final earnings ratio of 0.83 rather than the 0.88 that would have resulted had there been no amendments, thereby closing only 22 per cent of the overall wage gap as opposed to 44 per cent had there been no amendments. Because of the additional infusion of public funds to restore some of the old wage relativities, the overall cost was 8.8 per cent of the payroll, over twice the amount of the Minnesota adjustment.

9.5   OREGON: FROM COMPARABLE WORTH TO POVERTY RELIEF

In Oregon, the disputes amongst the various interest groups led to a shift in emphasis from conventional comparable worth to a policy of using the policy to provide poverty relief based on a given budgetary appropriation (Acker, 1989). The comparable worth initiative began through a feminist-led legislative proposal in 1981, that would have involved a broad application of comparable worth to all state employees. This legislation was not passed but led to a subsequent job evaluation in 1985 which determined that the female-dominated jobs were paid less than the male-dominated jobs of the same score by about 25 per cent at the unskilled entry level, and by about 10 per cent at the higher skill level, with no gap for the professional level jobs.

Disputes amongst the feminist contingent, the unions and management over technical issues precluded any agreement as to how to implement comparable worth. In 1987, the legislature subsequently passed pay equity legislation and appropriated a budget of US$22.6 million, leaving it up to the unions and management how to distribute the funds. After a strike and a fact-finding mission, the settlement involved distributing the funds disproportionately to the lowest paid groups which were also the most undervalued according to the job evaluation procedure.

The initial appropriation of US$22.6 million was distributed to 5,839 employees, which implies an average amount of US$3,870; however, this was not distributed all in one year and hence that average amount does not represent an increase in the base pay of those employees. The base pay increase essentially involved an increase in two salary steps of the lowest paid, most undervalued female-dominated jobs, and an increase of one salary step in the pay of the other undervalued female-dominated jobs. This led to increases respectively of 10 per cent and 5 per cent in the pay of these groups. Whether this would be permanent or temporary depends on what happens to those jobs in subsequent rounds of bargaining. These increases did not close the comparable worth wage gap, indicating how the emphasis shifted from conventional comparable worth to a policy of poverty relief.

9.6   SAN JOSE, CALIFORNIA

In San Jose[4] a series of comparable worth wage adjustments was instituted over the period 1981 to 1987, after a strike in 1981. The adjustments applied to 58 per cent of those female-dominated jobs that fell furthest below an overall pay line between pay and job evaluation points. They also applied only to those jobs represented by the union that led the strike.

The comparable worth wage adjustments occurred after a consultant's report in 1978 found that female-dominated jobs were paid 2 to 10 per cent below an overall comparable worth pay line (relating pay to points for all workers) while male-dominated jobs paid 8 to 15 per cent above the comparable worth line (Bunzel, 1982). This implies that female-dominated jobs were paid 10 to 25 per cent below male-dominated jobs of the same job evaluation score. A negotiated settlement was reached which involved US$1.4 million for 750 women over a two-year period. This implies an award of approximately US$1,900 per recipient in 1981-82.

Over the full implementation period from 1981 to 1987, Killingsworth (1990) finds that comparable worth by itself increased wages in female-dominated jobs by 5.8 per cent, after controlling for the other factors that also influenced wage growth. Comparable worth had no net effect on wages in male-dominated jobs. Kahn (1992) finds that over the implementation period, wages in the targeted jobs that received a comparable worth adjustment increased by 74 per cent while wages in the other jobs increased by only 50 per cent. She analysed other possible reasons for differences in this wage growth, and concluded that comparable worth was the main factor.

9.7 SIMULATIONS OF POTENTIAL IMPACT IN VARIOUS AMERICAN STATES

Sorensen (1986, 1987) provides simulation results of the estimated potential impact of comparable worth for a number of public sector cases in the United States, namely the states of Iowa, Michigan, Minnesota, Washington, and the city of San Jose, California. The results are not based on the actual wage adjustments in those particular cases. Rather, they are from simulations based on data on the wages and job evaluation scores. The simulations indicated the hypothetical wage increase that persons in female-dominated jobs could expect to receive if they were given the same pay as persons in male-dominated jobs of the same job evaluation score. Sorensen's results indicate that comparable worth wage increases ranging from 16 per cent to 34 per cent would occur depending upon the jurisdiction. The average increase was a little over 20 per cent. Such adjustments would increase the ratio of female-to-male earnings from 0.76 to 0.87, thereby closing approximately 45 per cent of the earnings gap in those particular cases. The overall cost is approximately 8 per cent of payroll.

Ehrenberg and Smith (1987) use a similar procedure for the states of Washington, Connecticut and Minnesota. They find that comparable worth wage increases would average slightly under 20 per cent if persons in female-dominated jobs were given the same pay as persons in male-dominated jobs of the same job evaluation score.

9.8 EXPERIENCE IN CANADIAN COMPLAINTS-BASED SYSTEMS

In the Canadian jurisdictions where complaints-based systems are in place, only a small number of complaints have been made.[5] When they did occur, however, the adjustments were quite substantial. For example, in 1980, 475 librarians each received a permanent adjustment averaging about Can.$2,000 per recipient with a one-time back pay award of that same magnitude. In 1982, approximately 3,300 general service workers received a permanent adjustment averaging about Can.$4,000. The adjustments based on raising the pay in undervalued female-dominated jobs to the male pay line have typically involved increases of 10 per cent or more.

9.9 MANITOBA: PROACTIVE APPLICATION TO THE PUBLIC SECTOR

In the proactive system in the province of Manitoba,[6] the magnitude of the average wage adjustment per recipient was similar to that occurring in the federal jurisdiction, albeit a much larger portion of the workforce received the adjustment. Specifically, the average annual wage adjustment for each employee who received an adjustment was approximately Can.$3,300 or a 15 per cent wage increase, ranging from 1 to 30 per cent. Approximately, one-third of the government's employees received the adjustment, increasing the overall payroll cost by about 3.3 per cent. The comparable worth adjustment increased the overall ratio of female-to-male wages from 0.82 prior to the adjustment to 0.87 after the adjustment, thereby closing slightly less than one-third (i.e. 0.05/0.18) of the overall wage gap. Two-thirds of the gap remained for two reasons: differences in the skill, effort, responsibility and working conditions between male- and female-dominated jobs; and the fact that many women were not eligible for wage adjustments because they were not employed in female-dominated jobs.

9.10 ONTARIO: PRIVATE AS WELL AS PUBLIC SECTOR APPLICATION

In the province of Ontario (where the impacts are likely to be most informative given the proactive application to both the public and the private sector) comprehensive information is not available as it was in many of the previously discussed cases. The public sector application in Ontario was not part of a single comprehensive application as in these other cases, but rather was done on a separate unit-by-unit basis, with the adjustment results generally not being publicly available. While the pay equity plans have to be posted within the organization, they do not have to be filed with the regulatory agency, the Pay Equity Commission; hence, there is not a central depository of the plans.

A number of documents give examples of settlements that have occurred in the proactive application in Ontario. Based on approximately 30 cases,[7] the average settlement was about Can.$4,400. Excluding the two highest and two lowest extremes or outliers as unrepresentative, the average was a little over Can.$4,000 or a 20 per cent wage increase. There was extreme variation, however, ranging from Can.$400 to $13,450. The settlements tended to be larger in the public sector than in the private sector and in unionized as opposed to non-unionized organizations.

Based on a survey[8] of public sector employers and large private sector employers with 500 or more employees, compliance was very poor as evidenced by the fact that almost a year after the required posting date only about half of the employers had posted their pay equity plans. For those organizations that made wage adjustments, in the public sector only about 38 per cent of employees in the female-dominated jobs received adjustments amounting to about 2.2 per cent of payroll. In the private sector, only about 18 per cent of employees in the female-dominated jobs received adjustments amounting to about 0.6 per cent of payroll. The lack of comparator groups probably accounts for a substantial portion of persons in female job classes not receiving an adjustment, and that this may account for some of the smaller payroll cost increases that have occurred in Ontario when compared to other proactive applications. In the other cases (e.g. Minnesota, Iowa, Manitoba) the application was generally done in a uniform, centralized fashion across the whole public sector, and comparator groups were either found or relationships were established by pay lines or other methods that did not require precise comparator groups.

With respect to private sector firms employing between 100 and 499 employers, compliance was also slow in terms of posting all their plans (Canadian Facts, 1992). With respect to wage adjustments, most female job classes received no adjustment. Specifically, in 79 per cent of the plans fewer than half of the female job classes received an adjustment, in 16 per cent of the plans over half but less than all of the female jobs received an adjustment, and in only 4 per cent of the plans did all of the female jobs receive an adjustment. The absence of adjustments was especially prominent in smaller, non-union establishments with a high proportion of females.

The overall cost of completing pay equity adjustment in such mid-sized private sector firms of between 100 and 499 employees was estimated by the employers as amounting to 1.1 per cent of their payroll costs. This is about twice the estimated cost of 0.6 per cent of payroll for larger private sector firms of 500 and more employees as discussed previously. Whether this reflects higher cost adjustments in the mid-sized firms, or a slower application in the larger firms, or simply differences in the way the data was compiled, is not known at this stage. What is safe to say, however, is that the adjustments in the private sector appear to amount to a smaller increase in payroll costs when compared to the public sector.

9.11   SUMMARY

- In complaints-based systems, only a small portion of the workforce tends to receive adjustments. In proactive, system-wide applications, which have taken place mainly in the public sector, larger portions of the workforce receive adjustments although even there considerable variation occurs depending upon the proportion of the workforce in female-dominated jobs, and the proportion of those who receive adjustments. When aggregated over a large public sector workforce, perhaps one-third of the total may be in female-dominated jobs. However, the proportion of those who receive an adjustment can vary anywhere from around 20 per cent to almost all incumbents of those jobs. It is this variation in "effective coverage" that gives rise to the substantial variation in payroll costs, even though the average adjustment for those who receive an adjustment is often fairly similar.

- In either complaints-based systems or proactive systems, when the adjustments occur, they tend to be quite large. While there is substantial, and often extreme, variation, adjustments in the neighbourhood of $4,000 (current US or Canadian dollars) are typical, amounting to wage increases of 10 to 20 per cent, usually closer to the latter.

- In the public sector workforces where these adjustments have usually been made, they typically raise the ratio of female-to-male earnings from 0.78 to 0.85 on average, thereby closing about one-third of the overall male-female wage gap within the organization. The remaining gap reflects a variety of factors. In the female-dominated jobs, there may be differences in skill, effort, responsibility and working conditions (i.e. in job evaluation points) when compared to the male-dominated jobs. Within the female-dominated jobs there may also be a lack of male comparators, and some males are in female-dominated jobs and hence receive an adjustment. Moreover, substantial numbers of women are employed in mixed or male-dominated jobs and hence do not receive an adjustment.

- While raising the ratio of female-to-male earnings from 0.78 to 0.85, and thereby closing about one-third of the wage gap, may be indicative of what happens to public sector workforces that undertake comparable worth, it may not be indicative of what would happen if comparable worth were applied throughout the economy as a whole. The public sector experience is not likely to be representative of what would happen in the private sector, and much of the aggregate wage gap arises because women are disproportionately employed in low wage establishments and industries while, conventionally, comparable worth is restricted to comparisons to within the same organization.

- In organizations that have implemented comparable worth, the adjustments have typically amounted to a cost of 4 to 8 per cent of the payroll. Considerably smaller payroll costs have been involved (e.g. 0.6 to 2.6 per cent) when only a small portion of the workforce in the organization has received an adjustment, usually because there are no male comparators or because no undervaluation was found.

– The limited amount of evidence that is available suggests that adjustment costs will be substantially smaller (e.g. 1 per cent or less of the payroll) in the private sector than in the public sector. This occurs both because smaller portions of the firm's workforce receive an adjustment and, when they do, it tends to be less in the private as opposed to the public sector.

Notes

[1] McCrudden (1991) reports a small number of cases in the United Kingdom where the comparable worth wage increases were in the neighbourhood of 10 to 20 per cent for recipients. These figures are in line with those reported here for the United States and Canada.

[2] The Washington State case is discussed in Evans and Nelson (1989), O'Neill, Brien, and Cunningham (1989), Remick (1984), and U.S. General Accounting Office (1992).

[3] The Minnesota experience is discussed in the Commission on the Economic Status of Women (1985), Evans and Nelson (1989) and Killingsworth (1990), as well as in references cited in those studies.

[4] The San Jose experience is analyzed in Kahn (1992) and Killingsworth (1990), as well as in references cited in those studies.

[5] This evidence is discussed in Gunderson (1989b, p. 220) and Gunderson and Riddell (1991, p. 165).

[6] The Manitoba experience is discussed in Gunderson and Riddell (1991), Manitoba Civil Service Commission (1988), and Weiner and Gunderson (1990).

[7] Calculations were done by the author based on the cases reported in the Ontario Pay Equity Commission (1991) and from the National Committee on Pay Equity (1990). The calculation of the overall average wage adjustment is not weighted by the number of recipients since such information was not always given. When only ranges of the wage increase were reported, the mid-point of that range was used. Hourly wages were converted to annual rates by multiplying by 2,000 hours, and weekly rates were multiplied by 50 weeks.

[8] SPR Associates Incorporated (1991).

EVIDENCE OF IMPACT ON WAGE GAP, EMPLOYMENT AND OTHER ASPECTS   **10**

While the previous "case studies" are informative in highlighting what has happened in those particular cases (usually in the public sector) where the policy has been applied, they do not indicate the effect that comparable worth could have on broader economy-wide aspects such as the overall male-female wage gap, or employment, or other dimensions such as wage structures or the attitudes of employees. These impacts are the focus of this chapter.

10.1   ECONOMETRIC STUDIES ON IMPACT ON OVERALL MALE-FEMALE WAGE GAP

A small number of econometric studies have attempted to provide an indication of the potential broader economy-wide application of comparable worth. The procedure essentially involves estimating a separate earnings equation for males and for females, based on the basic human capital and other determinants of earnings. Such human capital factors in the aggregate economy are regarded as proxies for the job evaluation scores that are relevant for comparable worth within organizations. The equations are usually estimated on large microeconomic data sets where the individual worker is the unit of observation. Each equation also includes a variable indicating the proportion of each worker's occupation that is female. The regression coefficient for that variable indicates the negative effect on the person's earnings of an increase in the proportion of their occupation that is female. The potential impact of comparable worth is simulated by eliminating the effect of the gender composition of the person's occupation on their wage. This is accomplished by setting the coefficient on that variable equal to zero and recalculating their earnings. Aggregating these across the individuals would give their hypothetical average earnings after comparable worth had eliminated the effect of the gender composition of their occupation on their earnings. The new hypothetical ratio of female-to-male earnings would give the expected earnings ratio after comparable worth is implemented, and from this one could calculate the portion of the overall earnings gap closed by comparable worth.

Simulations done in this fashion indicate that an economy wide application of comparable worth would close 8 to 20 per cent of the wage gap (Johnson and Solon, 1986) or 15 to 20 per cent of the wage gap (Aldrich and Buchele, 1986). The majority of the wage gap that would not be closed would reflect differences in the skill, effort, and responsibility between male- and female-dominated jobs, as well as differences in pay across establishments and industries, neither of which are within the scope of conventional comparable worth procedures.

10.2   ECONOMETRIC STUDIES OF THE EMPLOYMENT IMPACT

A small number of empirical studies have provided estimates of the employment effect of comparable worth. The methodologies usually involve estimating an employment-demand equation where employment is expressed as a function of wages and other control variables that may affect the demand for labour. These yield estimates of the elasticities of demand for labour indicating the percentage reduction in employment associated with a 1 per cent increase in wages. The expected employment impact of comparable worth is then simulated by multiplying the expected wage increase by the estimate of the elasticity of demand for labour.

Simulations for the public and private sectors

Based on American data for the *public* sector, Ehrenberg and Smith (1987a), simulate that a typical public sector comparable worth wage adjustment of 20 per cent would lead to only a 2 to 3 per cent reduction of employment in the female-dominated jobs. Aldrich and Buchele (1986) argue that comparable worth wage increases would likely be smaller in the *private* sector than in the public sector, nearer 10 to 15 per cent. Based on American data for the private sector, they estimate that such wage increases would lead to employment reductions of about 3 per cent.

Employment effects in San Jose, California and Minnesota

Based on data from the city of San Jose, California, Kahn (1992) finds that employment actually grew faster in the targeted female-dominated jobs that received the comparable worth wage adjustments. More specifically, over the implementation period, wages in targeted jobs increased by 74 per cent, compared to an increase of 50 per cent for other jobs. In spite of this more rapid wage increase in the targeted jobs, employment grew faster in those jobs than in other jobs. She also attributes much of this more rapid growth to a pro-female hiring policy that prevailed, spurred by affirmative action initiatives. This begs the question, of course, of whether employment growth would have been even more rapid were it not for the larger wage increases in the female-dominated jobs.

For San Jose, Killingsworth (1990) found that over the six-year implementation period from 1981 to 1987, comparable worth increased the wages in female-dominated jobs cumulatively by 5.8 per cent, and reduced female employment by a cumulative 6.6 per cent over that six-year period (i.e. by about 1 per cent per year).[1] His estimates indicate no effect on male pay and hence no effect on their employment. This cumulative effect on female employment is small when compared to the substantial overall increase in female employment that was occurring, averaging almost 10 per cent *per year*.

For state employees in Minnesota, Killingsworth (1990) estimated that over the three-year implementation period from 1983 to 1986 the cumulative wage gains from comparable worth to be 11.7 per cent for females and 1.8 per cent for males, with cumulative employment losses of 4.7 per cent for females and 1.2 per cent for males. These losses are less than the normal employment growth that occurred, being in the neighbourhood of 8 per cent for females and 10 per cent for males. This highlights that comparable worth led to slower employment growth but not absolute employment reductions.

Australian economy-wide experience

As discussed previously, the Australian experience is not of comparable worth in the conventional sense of organizations doing job evaluations and then adjusting wages in female-dominated jobs to the wages of male-dominated jobs of equal value. Nevertheless, the system of wage awards through tribunals did involve substantial wage increases to female-dominated occupations throughout the economy to remedy the past practice of official wage "markdowns" in those occupations. Since all organizations were affected, however, the employment effects may be smaller than those that would be experienced if the award only fell on one organization, which would then lose its market share relative to its competitors.

Gregory and Duncan (1981) estimate that the legislative increase in the ratio of female-to-male wages was associated with female employment growing faster than male employment, but the relative growth would have been even greater had it not been for the higher legislative wage increases. The adverse employment effect was larger in the private sector than in the public sector; in fact, there was no adverse employment effect in the public sector. Most of the adverse employment effect occurred as a result of a slower growth rate of female-dominated industries, and not because of a direct substitution of males or capital within each industry. While the adverse employment effect was statistically significant, Gregory and Duncan interpret it as being quantitatively small for such a large wage increase and improvement in the income share of women. In some updated work, Gregory and Duncan (1983) reiterate their conclusion. Killingsworth (1985) and McGavin (1983) both point out that there is a stronger adverse employment effect when measured in terms of hours of work rather than simply employment. That is, employers found it easier to cut back on hours of work rather making outright reductions in employment.

Based on an econometric model, Bonnell (1987) estimates the cumulative effects of comparable worth to reduce employment by about 6 per cent, slightly larger for females than males. The fact that both sexes experienced some employment reductions, and that male employment did not expand at the expense of female employment, suggests that the output effects, which lead to employment reductions for both sexes, were more prominent than any substitution of males for females. Killingsworth (1990) also referred to a number of other unpublished studies on the employment impact of comparable worth in Australia. Most confirmed that there was an adverse employment effect, but that it was small.

Killingsworth (1990) estimates the wage effect to be fairly substantial (up to 10 per cent in some specifications) over the first three years of the policy. These led to cumulative employment reductions of 5.2 per cent for all workers and 6.9 per cent for private sector workers. However, after the first three years of implementation, comparable worth ceased to have any independent effect on wages so that by ten years after the introduction of the policy the wage effects were essentially zero. As such, the adverse employment effects were also zero.

The Australian experience is still being debated (e.g. Gregory and Daly, 1991). Most studies tend to find that employment effects are negative but small, especially when such large wage increases occurred. If Killingsworth is correct, however, then the large wage increases would have occurred even without the comparable worth awards and therefore comparable worth had little or no independent impact on wages and hence employment. Whether this accounts for the small adverse employment effect found in the other studies (i.e. the *independent* wage effect of comparable worth in fact was small) is not known at this stage.

10.3   OTHER IMPACTS

While the wage and employment effects of comparable worth understandably receive the most attention, other impacts also occur, which have not been analysed systematically in the general literature on comparable worth; hence, they will be discussed here only in an illustrative fashion. The dimensions of these other impacts include: wage structures; occupational segregation; labour force participation and other more "general equilibrium" responses; administrative costs, especially associated with job evaluation; and attitudes of the different parties.

Wage structures

In addition to affecting the male-female wage structure, comparable worth can affect other wage structures. Based on American data, for example, Smith (1988) found that comparable worth actually widened the wage differential *within* the female workforce; that is, the gains went disproportionately to higher-wage women workers. This is a somewhat surprising result because one would normally expect that lower-wage women workers would disproportionately benefit because they are more likely to be in female-dominated jobs that would receive a positive adjustment, while higher-wage women workers are more likely to be in the higher paid male-dominated jobs that would not receive an adjustment. While this mechanism is at work, Smith found that it was overshadowed by the fact that higher-wage women workers in general were simply more likely to be covered by the legislation and hence eligible to receive its wage effects. Low-wage women workers in small private sector service establishments, for example, are simply not likely to be recipients of comparable worth adjustments, at least in so far as the law is currently structured. Comparable worth also reduces the economic returns to human capital formation in such forms as education, training and cumulative work experience (O'Neill, Brien and Cunningham, 1989; Orazem and Mattila, 1990).

Labour force participation

Based on a computable general equilibrium model of the American economy, Beider et al. (1988) provide simulation results indicating that comparable worth would increase the labour force participation rate and the employment of women, especially married women. This, in turn, would displace the employment of some males, especially single males, as well as single females.

Nakamura and Nakamura (1989) indicate that most estimates of the labour supply response of women, based on developed country data, suggest that wage increases will lead to substantial labour supply increases so that comparable worth could lead to substantial increases in the labour supply of women and thereby dampen their wage increases. However, they cite a number of studies, including their own work, which finds the labour supply response of women to a wage increase to be negligible, and more like that of men. To the extent that this is true, then comparable worth would not alter their labour supply and hence it would not lead to any subsequent dampening effect on their wages.

Administrative cost

Robb (1987, p. 149) cites Canadian evidence from the mid-1980s indicating that job evaluation procedures exist in 67 per cent of large firms of over 1,000 employees, in 70 per cent of medium-sized firms of 200 to 999 employees, and in 50 per cent of smaller firms with 50 to 199 employees. However, only a little over half of these are suitable for comparable worth purposes. More specifically, the proportion of firms with job evaluation procedures that can be used for comparable worth purposes is 48 per cent for large firms, 36 per cent for medium-sized firms and 21 per cent for smaller firms. The administrative cost of setting up a job evaluation procedure was between Can.$300 and Can.$500 per employee for small firms, and between Can.$200 and Can.$300 per employee for large firms.

Employers who developed pay equity plans under the Ontario proactive legislation were asked to estimate the "administrative cost of developing their plan". Since the job evaluation procedure was not explicitly mentioned, it is not clear whether this would also include those costs. The administrative costs per employee were estimated at Can.$173 for public sector employers, Can.$88 for large private sector employers of 500 or more employees (SPR Associates, 1991, p. 40), and Can.$168 for smaller private sector employers of 100 to 499 employees (Canadian Facts, 1992, p. 45). These are likely to be lower bound estimates since they may not include the job evaluation costs, which were considerably higher as indicated above. Approximating the average administrative cost of getting such an adjustment as Can.$150, and if 20 per cent of employees receive an adjustment, then the average cost per recipient of an award would be Can.$750. If the average magnitude of each award was Can.$4,000, then it would cost Can.$0.19 per dollar of transfer payment that is involved in the award. That is, the administrative cost of providing redress is about 20 per cent of the cost of the redress itself.

Attitudes of the parties

From their survey of state government employees in Minnesota, Evans and Nelson (1989) report that 59 per cent felt it would lead to wage reductions or wage freezes for some groups. In spite of that perception, 64 per cent felt that the policy did not cause any problems at the workplace, and this figure was similar for male and female respondents. Their most surprising result, however, is that 43 per cent of employees who received a comparable worth wage adjustment were unaware that they had received one, in spite of the fact that the average adjustment was US$2,200 per recipient. This leads them to state: "The social movement potential of comparable worth is certainly unfulfilled if 43.2 per cent of the people who benefit from the policy are unaware of their benefits." This lack of knowledge is particularly disconcerting since they also found that the employees who were most satisfied with their jobs were those who received an adjustment and who knew that they had received one, and those who were least satisfied with their jobs were those who received an adjustment but were not aware that they had received one.

Evans and Nelson (1986) point out that this lack of information, paradoxically, was a conscious policy on the part of the union, as the awards were not announced and were added incrementally to paychecks. The union was concerned that general knowledge of the awards may engender opposition from those who did not receive an award. Moreover, if announced as a pay equity adjustment, "credit" may go to management for making the adjustment. Otherwise, the union may get credit if it appeared as part of the results of normal collective bargaining. Presumably, management went along with not publicizing the results, perhaps so as not to alienate the union, and management may also have been concerned with the reaction of those who did not receive an award.

Based on the proactive experience in Ontario, SRP Associates (1991) and Canadian Facts (1992) reported that slightly over half of the employers claimed that the policy had no effect on morale. Of those who reported an impact, a negative impact was more common. This negative impact was especially pronounced in the large public sector organizations (e.g. 40 to 45 per cent of public sector organizations with over 100 employees reported a negative impact, with only 14 per cent reporting a positive impact). For issues such as communication around compensation issues, employee understanding of pay equity, and perceptions of fairness between male and female jobs, the most common response was also that pay equity had no significant effect. However, for those who perceived it to have an impact, a positive one was more common than a negative impact. The main exception was for the perceived impact on personnel systems, which was most commonly viewed as positive, then as having no effect, and with very few responding that it had a negative impact.

10.4   SUMMARY

- Simulation results for the economy as a whole suggest that an economy-wide application of comparable worth would close 8 to 20 per cent of the wage gap. The majority of the wage gap would not be closed, reflecting differences in the skill, effort, responsibility and working conditions between male- and female-dominated jobs, as well as the fact that many women are employed in mixed or male-dominated jobs. Furthermore, the overall gap in the economy as a whole reflects differences in pay across establishments and industries, neither of which are within the scope of conventional comparable worth procedures.

- There is considerable controversy about the employment impacts of comparable worth. Most studies suggest that the adverse employment effect would be small because employers would not greatly reduce their employment growth in jobs that received the wage increases, in spite of the fact that the wage increases are fairly substantial. Some studies, however, find the adverse employment effect to be small simply because the independent impact of comparable worth on wages is calculated to be small. Others find moderate impacts on both wages and employment growth. In all cases, however, any adverse employment effect occurs in the form of slower employment growth rather than in the form of absolute employment reductions, since overall employment growth has tended to be substantial for women. Alternatively stated, any reduction in employment growth has tended to be small relative to the general growth of female employment that has occurred.

– Some limited evidence suggests that comparable worth may widen the wage differential *within* the female workforce, largely because higher-wage women workers are more likely to receive a wage adjustment and low-wage women workers are unlikely to be covered at all.

– Even though higher pay is given for higher job evaluation points related to such factors as skill and responsibility, comparable worth appears to lead to some reduction in the economic returns to human capital formation in such forms as education, training and work experience.

– Some limited evidence suggests that the administrative costs associated with comparable worth are not inconsequential. Costs in the neighbourhood of Can.$150 per employee have been cited. If 20 per cent of employees receive an adjustment, this implies a cost of Can.$750 *per recipient*, or 20 per cent of the average award of Can.$4,000.

– In the state of Minnesota, almost half of those who received a comparable worth adjustment were unaware that they had received an adjustment, in spite of the fact that the average adjustment was US$2,200.

– Some limited evidence suggests that comparable worth usually has no significant positive or negative impact on morale, although when it had an impact, the negative impact was slightly more common than the positive impact. For issues such as communication around compensation issues, employees' understanding of pay equity, and perceptions of fairness between male and female jobs, the most common perception was also one of no significant effect. However, for those who perceived it to have an impact, a positive impact was more common than a negative impact for these issues. The main exception was for the perceived impact on personnel systems, which was most commonly viewed as positive (Gunderson and Riddell, 1988, p. 171).

Notes

[1] The elasticity of demand for labour is the percentage change in employment that results from a 1 per cent increase in wages. Typical elasticities are in the neighborhood of -0.33, indicating that a 1 per cent increase in wages leads to a one-third of 1 per cent reduction in employment.

APPLICATION TO THE PRIVATE SECTOR

11

At the outset it should be emphasized that there is nothing *theoretically* wrong or inappropriate about applying the concept of comparable worth to the private sector, if it is deemed an appropriate concept in the first place. The principle is as valid in the private sector as it is in the public sector. However, as discussed in this chapter, in practice the implementation problems may be quite different and the present-day applications to the private sector have been extremely restricted.

11.1 CURRENT APPLICATION TO THE PRIVATE SECTOR

The international initiatives in the area of comparable worth apply to the private sector as well as to the public sector. The ILO Equal Remuneration Convention (No. 100), which requires ratifying countries to promote the policy of equal pay for work of equal value, applies to both the private and public sectors. However, in providing guidelines on implementing the policy, the Equal Remuneration Recommendation (No. 90) does make a distinction in its application in the public and private sectors. Specifically, it states that the central government should *ensure* its application to employees of the central government, and *encourage* its application to employees of other levels of government. With respect to the private sector, the government is to provide for the legal enactment of the general application of comparable worth.

At the international level, the Equal Pay Directive of 1975 for the European Economic Community also envisages the application of the principle of comparable worth to the private as well as the public sector. Although this general legal requirement exists, it is left up to individual member countries as to how they will implement the requirement. In countries where there is a high degree of centralized bargaining, the general legal requirement has usually led to the incorporation of the principle into the bargaining process, but it is difficult to tell if it is being applied on a regular basis in practice. Certainly, it is not being applied to the private sector in a systematic proactive fashion involving all of the implementation steps of proactive application.

Individual complaints in such situations of centralized collective bargaining are also rare. They are also relatively rare, however, in decentralized systems such as in those Canadian and American jurisdictions that rely on complaints-based enforcement. This highlights a difficulty with the application of comparable worth in the private sector. The complex nature of the implementation process makes it difficult to bring forth a complaint, let alone to know if a complaint is appropriate in the first place. Individuals usually know if they are sexually harassed, or denied a job or promotion opportunity because of their gender, or if they are not receiving the same pay for the same work done by a male co-worker. However, prior to any gender-neutral job evaluation procedure, it is difficult for them to know if their job is undervalued in terms of skill, effort, responsibility and working conditions, relative to some completely different job.

In Australia, the application of comparable worth to the private sector was facilitated by its unusual system of centralized wage determination through the central and regional tribunals that make wage awards. The process essentially involved the removal of official "markdowns" that previously existed in female-dominated jobs.

In the United States, where the policy of comparable worth was first instituted, it is largely a public sector phenomenon. Legislative application in the private sector is virtually non-existent.

In Canada, where the implementation of comparable worth has gone furthest, it is also largely a public sector phenomenon. In theory, in jurisdictions that have complaints-based enforcement, the policy does apply to the private sector. However, in practice its application has been to the public sector. Where enforcement has been through proactive system-wide application, the policy has largely been restricted to the public sector. The notable exception is in Ontario, where the policy is being applied to the private sector in a proactive fashion.

11.2   POTENTIAL IMPACT IN THE PRIVATE SECTOR

The *potential scope* for comparable worth is likely to be greater in the private sector than in the public sector, in part because the productivity-adjusted earnings gap tends to be greater in the private sector than in the public sector (Gunderson, 1989a). While the wage gap is likely to be greater in the private sector than in the public sector, the resistance to closing that gap is also likely to be greater in the private sector. Public sector wage determination is influenced extensively by political constraints, as well as by institutional features (binding wage arbitration, high degree of unionization) that facilitate the operation of those political constraints. If the political pressures, prompted by legislation, are to institute comparable worth, then there is little resistance to the policy.

In contrast, in the private sector, the profit constraint replaces the political constraint of the public sector as the operative pressure for wage determination. Resistance to comparable worth wage increases thereby is likely to be greater in the private sector, since they are seen directly as costs, with little or no "political benefits". The cost concerns are likely to be particularly strong under increasing global competition and international trade, since price increases can lead to substantial losses of markets to foreign competitors. Moreover, with the increasing mobility of financial and physical capital, high costs may make it more difficult to attract investments.

This greater cost sensitivity in the private sector suggests that the comparable worth wage adjustments will be smaller in the private sector than in the public sector, in spite of the fact that the comparable worth wage gap is likely to be larger in the private than in the public sector. The greater cost sensitivity also suggests that any adverse employment effect for a given wage increase is also likely to be larger in the private sector than in the public sector.

11.3   EVIDENCE ON IMPACT IN THE PRIVATE SECTOR

Given the limited application of comparable worth in the private sector, it is not surprising that there is little evidence on its actual impact in that sector. Nevertheless, as discussed previously, there is some evidence that can shed light on its likely impact if it is expanded more broadly to the private sector.

If it is expanded on the basis of complaints-based enforcement, it is unlikely to affect a substantial portion of the workforce largely because complaints are rare, given the complications of the procedure. Cases that are settled, however, are likely to lead to substantial wage adjustments for recipients and this may have spillover effects to other workers.

If the principle of comparable worth is incorporated into the principle of centralized bargaining or wage determination, then it can have a larger impact throughout the private sector. Such procedures, however, usually do not involve comparable worth in the conventional sense of its basic steps. Rather, the process tends to involve making larger wage awards in female-dominated jobs to achieve a greater degree of equity between male and female workers. These procedures seem to have been reasonably successful at increasing the pay in female-dominated jobs and thereby reducing the overall wages gap, albeit there can be some dispute (as is the case in Australia) over the independent long-term impact of a conscious comparable worth policy. Of course, this procedure would not work in countries with decentralized wage-determination processes, as is the case in the United States and Canada.

With respect to the possible adverse employment effects from broader scale application of comparable worth wage increases in the private sector, the most extensive empirical evidence comes from Australia. Even if the wage increases are better thought of as emanating from tribunal wage-fixing machinery, rather than conventional comparable worth, the fact remains that substantial wage increases did go to the female-dominated jobs and this should provide an indication of the potential employment impact of comparable worth. Unfortunately, as discussed previously, there is substantial disagreement over the magnitude of that adverse employment effect. Some interpret it as being very small for such large wage increases. Others argue that it is larger when reductions in hours of work are considered, and when the focus is on the private sector. Some also argue that the long-term employment impact was small because, in the long run, comparable worth did not have much of an independent impact on wages in the first place.

As discussed previously, simulation results for the United States indicate that the adverse employment effect of a given magnitude of a comparable worth wage increase would be larger in the private sector (Aldrich and Buchele, 1986) than in the public sector (Ehrenberg and Smith, 1987). This is a direct result of the larger employment elasticity estimated for the private sector compared to the public sector. The comparable worth wage increases themselves were expected to be smaller in the private sector. Combining the smaller wage increase with a greater employment response to a given increase yielded an employment reduction of around 3 per cent in the private sector, compared to 2 to 3 per cent in the public sector. In either case, the employment responses were perceived to be small.

Perhaps the best evidence of the expected impact of comparable worth in the private sector compared to the public sector will come from the Ontario experience, given its proactive application to both sectors in that province. Unfortunately, systematic evidence of that impact is not available. The limited evidence discussed previously, however, suggests that the adjustment costs will be substantially smaller in the private sector, leading to overall payroll cost increases of around 1 per cent of payroll. This is substantially smaller than the 4 to 8 per cent of payroll found in many other proactive applications in the public sectors of other jurisdictions, and the 2 to 3 per cent increases that are occurring in public sector organizations in Ontario. The smaller impact in the private sector occurred both because a smaller portion of the private sector firm's workforce received wage adjustments, and because the wage adjustments themselves tended to be smaller. The extent to which these results reflect specific aspects of the Canadian application (e.g. the chance to do nothing when there are no comparator jobs) remains unknown.

11.4 IMPLEMENTATION PROBLEMS IN THE PRIVATE SECTOR .

While in theory, the principle of comparable worth is as appropriate in the private sector as in the public sector, in practice the implementation problems, which are already severe in the public sector, are likely to be even more severe in the private sector. This is true for each and every step in the implementation of comparable worth.

The most important ingredient in the first step of identifying gender-dominated jobs, is to have a sufficient number of male-dominated jobs for meaningful comparison purposes. This may be a problem, especially in small private sector establishments. Small-scale employers may also be able to circumscribe the legislation by manipulating a few key job incumbents to make comparisons more difficult or to make the wage adjustments smaller.

The second step in comparable worth involves evaluating the worth of jobs through job evaluation procedures. This is more difficult for the private sector than for the public sector because job evaluation procedures are less common in the private sector, and when they do exist they are often not suitable for comparable worth purposes.

The third step in implementing comparable worth involves relating pay to the value of the job, where the value is determined by comparable worth procedures. If pay lines are estimated, then a sufficient number of jobs are needed for accurate estimation of the lines. If specific job-to-job comparisons are used, then a sufficient number of jobs is necessary to find male comparator jobs of the same value. For smaller private sector employers this problem of lack of male-dominated comparator jobs is more likely to occur, and when it does occur, it is not as likely to be amenable to solutions such as broadening the definition of the employer.

The fourth step in implementing comparable worth involves adjusting the pay in undervalued female-dominated jobs to the pay of the male comparator jobs. Probably the simplest procedure for doing so is to adjust to a male pay line, either by adjusting an estimated female pay line to the male pay line, or by raising the pay in each undervalued female-dominated job to the male pay line. However, the estimating of pay lines is not likely to be a viable option in small private sector firms, given the small number of jobs involved.

11.5 CONCLUDING OBSERVATIONS ON PRIVATE SECTOR APPLICATION

Implementation problems, which are already severe in the public sector, will be even more severe in the private sector, for each and every step in the implementation process. This is especially the case for small private sector employers where male comparator jobs may be fewer and where job evaluations suitable for comparable worth will be less common.

These problems suggest that special attention must be paid to the application of comparable worth to the private sector, especially to smaller employers. The issue is especially severe because the small business sector is increasingly regarded as a crucial engine of economic growth and job creation. It is important that regulatory costs do not discourage the involvement of women in that growth and job creation. It is also important, however, that they participate in that job creation in a fair and equitable fashion. For these reasons attention should be paid to design issues such as phasing and cost ceilings, as well as to the possibility of providing assistance with implementation in the private sector. Also, attention should be paid to alternative policies for achieving the same or similar ends in the private sector.

COMPARABLE WORTH
IN DIFFERENT ECONOMIC SYSTEMS
AND DEVELOPMENT STAGES

12

The discussion so far has been based on the application of comparable worth mainly in the United States and Canada, since, so far, the procedure has been applied most extensively in these countries and most of the evaluations have been done there. The application of the principle of equal pay in Australia is characterized by wage fixing through arbitration tribunals, rather than by conventional equal pay with job evaluation and other comparable worth steps. While this has certainly been the case, there is now a shift in wage-fixing arrangements towards a much greater focus on workplace bargaining. The Australian Industrial Relations Commission has established a new enterprise bargaining principle which allows for wage rises to be negotiated between unions and employers in return for productivity changes at the workplace level. These arrangements are underpinned by an enforceable award framework with classifications established on a comparative work value basis, which is being undertaken as part of a review of award wage relativities (a process called the minimum rates adjustment (MRA) process). The aim of the MRA process is to ensure that work performed under individual award classifications is valued appropriately in comparison with benchmark classifications and with classifications within the same award – on the basis of skill, responsibility, and the conditions under which the work is normally performed.

Previously, in Chapter 9, the legal and institutional arrangements for applying comparable worth in North America were analysed. This chapter focuses on the issues associated with the application of comparable worth to countries with different economic systems, development stages and employment practices. The focus is on the implications of the key aspects of these different economic systems for the application of comparable worth. Are there aspects of these different economic systems and development stages that make the concept of comparable worth inappropriate as a policy? Are there aspects that make it more difficult or easier to implement the policy? Are there aspects that make it such that alternative policies would be more effective in achieving the same goals?

A comprehensive analysis of the application of comparable worth to a wide range of specific countries is beyond the scope of this analysis. The purpose is not to do a country-by-country analysis of how comparable worth has been implemented. Rather, the focus is on selecting a small number of generic economic systems and development stages that illustrate the issues. When specific countries are discussed, it is to illustrate the issues associated with the particular generic economic system and development stage of which they are representative.

The different economic systems and development stages that will be analysed here are: the European Community; Japanese-style labour markets; the newly industrializing countries with a relatively large urban formal sector; and the developing countries with a large urban informal sector and a large rural traditional subsistence sector. For each system, the key characteristics will be identified along with their implications for the application of the principle of comparable worth.

12.1 EUROPEAN COMMUNITY

The economic system of the European Community (EC) is most like that of North America in the sense that both are advanced industrialized economies with common concerns over issues like inflation, unemployment, growth, inequality and international competitiveness. In spite of these similarities, there are substantial differences between the EC and the United States that have important implications for the implementation of comparable worth.

European Community countries are more likely to attempt a "collective response" to social problems, in comparison to the emphasis on individual rights enforced through litigation that tends to characterize much of American social policy. With respect to comparable worth, this suggests that EC countries would be more prone to achieve the broad goals of comparable worth by incorporating them into existing institutional arrangements such as centralized bargaining with unions or as part of an egalitarian wage policy. There may also be more tendency to explore alternative mechanisms such as minimum wages or wage extension by decree. These would be emphasized over the mechanisms of litigation and individual complaints.

Although the impact of national or regional wage agreements varies from one country to another, wage determination within the different countries of the EC tends to be more centralized, often with unions having an important say in the determination of the "social wage". As such, there is more scope to increase the wages of female-dominated jobs through this process of centralized bargaining. While gender discrimination is not a main focus in wage negotiations, in some instances women's wages have received preferential treatment, more as a result of a general egalitarian policy than as a result of any anti-discriminatory policy.

While centralized bargaining provides the potential to increase wages in female-dominated jobs without having to go through all of the complex steps of conventional enterprise level implementation, it also has the potential to ignore this issue in the political tradeoffs that tend to characterize such bargaining. Individual complaints may also be more difficult to deal with, as evidenced by the fact that they tend to be less common in such systems of centralized bargaining. Furthermore, without the conventional implementation steps, the redress may be less targeted to the specific female-dominated jobs that are most undervalued.

To a large degree, the efficacy of attaining the objectives of comparable worth through more centralized bargaining depends upon one's perspective on the objectives of comparable worth. If the objective is to increase the pay in female-dominated jobs because they have been systematically undervalued, and comparable worth is simply regarded as one of many mechanisms to achieve that objective, then centralized bargaining is likely to become a more effective instrument than the conventional steps of comparable worth to achieve that broad goal. However, if the goal is to eliminate unequal pay for work of equal value within each organization, then the conventional comparable worth steps are likely to be more effective and targeted.

While job evaluation for the purpose of establishing wage grading in enterprises is fairly common, formal, analytical job evaluation techniques that are conducive to applying comparable worth at the decentralized, enterprise level are not common (with the exception of Germany, the Netherlands and the United Kingdom). The emphasis on centralized, industry-wide bargaining does not always rely on such techniques. This makes the conventional application of comparable worth more difficult (because of the lack of job evaluation), but also possibly less necessary if the goals can be incorporated into the more centralized bargaining procedures.

The EC countries also have the mechanism of the Social Charter of 1989 to help achieve broader social objectives across the member countries.[1] The Social Charter is intended to encourage a degree of uniformity of standards with respect to social policy and labour regulations. One purpose is to prevent "social dumping" whereby countries compete on the basis of low labour standards as a way of keeping labour costs down. Without the greater degree of uniformity of legislated standards, market forces may lead to downward harmonization as countries compete to attract investment or to reduce the regulatory component of labour cost. The Social Charter is designed to prevent such downward harmonization, and to possibly encourage upward harmonization.

What is not known is the extent to which progress in achieving the goals of comparable worth has been made by incorporating the principles into the process of centralized bargaining. Treu (1986, p. 25) states: "using a relatively centralized bargaining structure to implement wage policy has faster and more diffusive effects than following a case-by-case approach based on plant-wide job evaluation practices or court action." He also states (p. 30), however, that "A diffusion of centralized directives, through the various channels and the decentralized initiatives of the various labour relations actors, is essential for real and lasting changes in the complicated area of wage structures and pay equity to occur."

While the principle of comparable worth is fairly entrenched in the legal apparatus of the EC, it does not seem to be extensively applied in practice, at least not in the conventional form at the enterprise level based on job evaluation techniques. In essence, its strict implementation does not seem to have been absorbed into the wage determination of most EC countries. As stated by Treu, (1986, p. 13): "When the other [non-UK] EEC members finally did legislate, they limited themselves to literally reproducing the directive's substantive contents, resulting in a technical compliance with the directive which was not a fully conscious or convinced acceptance." Or as more strongly stated by Ephron (1986, p. 206): "Although at this date most of the Member States have implemented legislation in order to comply with the 1975 Directive, it is clear that those countries that have chosen to reiterate equal pay guarantees as enunciated in the Directive, without actually considering the actual process of implementing the guarantee, have not fulfilled their obligation nor closed the debate. A guarantee that provides equal pay for work of equal value is an empty promise in a country where the methods and assumptions used in attributing value to a job have not been thoroughly discussed."

12.2 JAPANESE-STYLE LABOUR MARKETS[2]

Issues of gender discrimination have not been paramount in Japanese labour law. There have been few court cases and all have been on conventional equal pay within the same job, and not on comparable worth comparisons across different jobs. Issues of efficiency and growth have dominated concern over issues of equity and fairness. Tradition is strong, and women traditionally have a strong role in the household and a weaker role in the labour market. As a result, a large gender pay gap persists in Japan (ILO, Report of the Committee of Experts on the Application of Conventions and Recommendations, 1992 and 1993; Mori, 1992).

Many of the characteristics of Japanese-style labour markets make the application of comparable worth difficult. Rather than being employed in the larger establishments that provide high wages and "life-time" employment, women in Japan have traditionally been employed in sectors that are less amenable to legislative protection. These include agriculture, self-employment in family businesses, and employment in smaller establishments and in part-time work with subcontractors. In Japan, job evaluation is not common even in the larger establishments. Rather, wages tend to be determined by education and seniority. Although it is changing somewhat, women tend not to acquire education that is labour-market oriented, and they tend not to accumulate continuous seniority because of the tradition of leaving the labour force for child-raising, and returning subsequently to part-time work.

Determining the overall pay that people receive can be difficult because of the different components that are involved, a factor that is important in most countries, but especially so in Japan. The components of compensation include: the basic wage (based on seniority and merit); supplements for the particular job and function; allowances for housing and commuting; payments for overtime work and night work; and bonuses and retirement payments. Many of these components can be accommodated and dealt with under comparable worth. They make implementation more difficult, but not impossible.

12.3   NEWLY INDUSTRIALIZING COUNTRIES[3]

With respect to the application of labour policies, it is important to make a distinction between the newly industrializing countries (NICs) and the developing countries (DCs). The NICs tend to have a higher level of development and are closer to the industrialized country model. While wages in the NICs are typically considerably less than wages in the more industrialized countries, they are considerably higher than wages in the developing countries, and in fact are often converging towards the wages of the industrialized countries with which they increasingly trade. Moreover, while they may have an informal urban sector and a pool of rural labour that can potentially flood the formal, urban labour market, that informal sector is considerably smaller in the NICs than in the DCs. In whatever sector they work (i.e. urban formal, urban informal, or rural subsistence), women tend to bear the additional burden or "tax" of household responsibilities which, in turn, can affect their labour market activity (Palmer, 1991, p. 12). Examples of NICs include Brazil, the Republic of Korea, Mexico, Singapore, and Taiwan, China.

Similarities between NICs and developed countries

The NICs share a number of characteristics with their more industrial counterparts, at least with respect to the modern, urban sector of the developing economies. Male-female wage differentials are prominent, and reflect both differences in human capital endowments as well as discrimination. The discriminatory components reflect both wage discrimination (wage differences for the same endowments of wage-determining characteristics) as well as occupational segregation. With respect to the organization of work, these similarities include: relatively large enterprises; formalized work arrangements; specialization and delineation of tasks; fixed hours of work; and a separation of work arrangements from the home.

These similarities in the determinants of the male-female pay gap suggest that there is a potential role for comparable worth policies in the NICs, just as there is in the more developed countries. The occupational segregation means that conventional policies of equal pay for equal work will not be sufficient because of their inability to make comparisons across different jobs in different occupations. Comparable worth policies can involve such comparisons. Whether they would be more effective than equal employment opportunity policies or affirmative action programmes which could reduce occupational segregation is an open question, just as it is in the more industrialized countries.

The similarities with respect to how work is organized also suggest the feasibility of applying comparable work. The importance of large enterprises means that job evaluation procedures can be utilized and it will be easier to find male-comparator jobs. Formalized work arrangements, the specialization and delineation of tasks, and the separation of work arrangements from the home, facilitates determining the "value" of the different jobs. The fixed hours of work facilitate comparisons of pay on a comparable basis per unit of time.

The formal, urban sector in the NICs often consists, to a substantial extent, of public sector jobs. As discussed previously, the implementation of comparable worth is easier in the public sector than in the private sector. Even many of the private sector jobs in the formal, urban labour market are jobs in the large multinational corporations that are likely to have experience with comparable worth in other countries in which they operate.

These similarities between NICs and their industrial counterparts with respect to such factors as the determinants of the pay gap and the nature of work arrangements suggest that comparable worth policies are both relevant and feasible. They also suggest, however, that the same practical implementation issues will be experienced in the NICs as well as in the more developed countries.

Differences that emphasize other policies

While there are these similarities between the developing and the more developed economies that suggest both the relevance and feasibility of comparable worth, there are also some important differences that have implications for such policies. Comparable worth policies were designed to deal with systemic discrimination that is often the unintended by-product of other personnel policies and practices. Discrimination in the developing countries tends to be more overt, with all parties (employers, males and even females) often adhering to traditional attitudes about what jobs are "suitable and proper" for women, and what pay is "appropriate" given perceptions about who is the "breadwinner".

This does not negate the relevance and feasibility of comparable worth, but it does highlight the importance of more basic policies such as equal employment opportunity legislation and conventional equal pay legislation that are designed to deal with the more overt forms of discrimination. It also highlights the importance of changing the attitudes (many of which emanate from outside of the labour market) that give rise to and sustain such practices at the workplace.

Differences that can be dealt with by comparable worth

Any differences between the NICs and their more developed counterparts in such factors as male-female differences in education, absenteeism, turnover, and willingness to take on supervisory responsibility should not pose a major problem in the implementation of comparable worth since they can all be incorporated into the compensable factors of skill, effort, responsibility and working conditions that constitute the value of a job. Both the level and type of education, for example, would enter the skill component if it is relevant to the job. Physical strength would enter the category of effort, and supervisory responsibility would obviously enter the category of responsibility. Of course, these categories may be given inappropriate weights and gender biases may exist in the job evaluation procedure itself, but these are problems that are common to job evaluation procedures whether they are applied in developed or newly industrialized countries.

While these issues do not pose a basic problem with the implementation of comparable worth, they do magnify the usual implementation problems because there are simply more differences to evaluate and hence to be subject to contentious debate. For example, if physical strength matters, then there is more need to be concerned over whether it is properly measured or given the appropriate weight in job evaluation procedures. If there are more substantial differences in the value of the jobs as measured by the inputs of skill, effort, responsibility and working conditions between the male-dominated and female-dominated jobs in newly industrialized countries when compared to the more developed countries, this also suggests that there will be fewer male-dominated jobs of the same value as many of the female-dominated jobs. This will make equal value comparisons more difficult and compound the issue of what to do when there are insufficient male comparators. There may also be less acceptance of a procedure like comparable worth if there are strong perceptions about differences in the nature of the work done by men and women.

Differences that are difficult to incorporate into comparable worth

While differences in such factors as education, physical strength and supervisory responsibility can readily be incorporated into the compensable factors in job evaluation procedures, this is not always the case with respect to other factors. Differences in absenteeism, for example, are not easily accommodated into job evaluation procedures because they tend to be specific to the individual worker, while job evaluation evaluates jobs and not people. For example, two individuals in the same job would get the same job evaluation score even if one had higher absenteeism than the other. Of course, if the absenteeism became a major obstacle to carrying on the basic functions of the job, then presumably the individual could be reassigned to another job perhaps with less responsibility (and hence a lower job evaluation score) because absenteeism matters in terms of the responsibility of the job. Nevertheless, this would most likely rarely occur, in which case differences in such factors as absenteeism would not be fully accounted for in conventional job evaluation procedures.

This could also be the case with respect to differences in expected cost associated with such factors as turnover, maternity leave and so-called "protective legislation" such as prohibitions on night work done by women. The latter, especially, may be more prominent in newly industrialized countries because of traditional views of the need to "protect" women. In more developed countries, special protective legislation for women tends to be viewed as either unnecessary given the changing role of women in society, or even as counterproductive to women, because it enhances the image of women as the "weaker sex", or it adds to the cost of employing women and hence "protects" male jobs.

12.4   DEVELOPING COUNTRIES

Relative to the newly industrialized countries, the developing countries (DCs) have lower levels of industrial development, wages, capital/labour ratios and levels of unionization. Most importantly for the application of comparable worth, they have a smaller formal, urban sector and a much larger informal urban sector as well as a much larger rural, traditional, subsistence, sector. The informal urban sector tends to involve characteristics such as: non-fixed worksites; self-employment or piece-rate work; small enterprises sometimes within the household; informal work arrangements; and non-fixed hours of work.

The formal urban sector of developing countries has many characteristics of the formal urban sector of the NICs. As such, the same issues apply with respect to the applicability of comparable worth, that is, it has a potential role to play and many of the differences between the developing countries and more developed countries can be accommodated in the procedures of comparable worth. However, that role is severely circumscribed by many of the differences between the developing countries and their more developed counterparts, differences that make the implementation of an already complex policy even more difficult. Furthermore, resistance to such a complex policy may be strong to the extent that its cost implications impede the development process. There also appears to be greater potential scope for more basic anti-discrimination policies, such as equal employment opportunity policies and education and other policies outside of the labour market.

While these same issues apply to developing countries as well as to the more advanced NICs, they are more especially relevant to developing countries, given their earlier stage in the development process. Furthermore, the prominence of the informal urban sector and the rural subsistence sector in developing countries has important implications for the applicability of comparable worth. First, the policy obviously cannot be applied in those sectors; it is a policy that is potentially relevant only for the formal sector given the steps that are involved in implementing comparable worth. Secondly, the rural sector and the informal urban sector are a primary source of labour supply to the formal urban sector. As such the integration of women into the labour market could probably be best fostered by policies to facilitate their transition from the rural or the informal urban sector into the formal urban sector on an equitable and non-discriminatory basis. Additionally, the potential scope is greatest for more basic policies like equal pay and equal employment opportunity legislation, as well as initiatives outside of the labour market.

Thirdly, the presence of the rural sector and the informal urban sector means that there is a constant potential pool of labour, often flooding the formal urban labour market and leading to high levels of unemployment. This does not mean that efforts should not be made to reduce the effects of discrimination in the formal sector simply because there is a potential pool of women willing to do those jobs even under discriminatory conditions. Such queues are present for all jobs in the formal sector of developing countries, and in fact are often present for the developed countries given the pools of unemployed workers and household labour. It does mean, however, that any comparable worth wage increases in the formal urban sector would make those jobs even more coveted and this would increase the already large number of persons vying for those jobs. Furthermore, cost increases in those jobs may reduce the number of such jobs. This in turn may close off one of the important channels for women obtaining well-paid jobs in the formal urban sector.

12.5 SUMMARY OF APPLICABILITY IN DIFFERENT ECONOMIC SYSTEMS

In the market-oriented systems of the United States and Canada (where comparable worth has been most extensively applied) a number of conditions prevail that facilitate its application. There is considerable experience with anti-discrimination law and litigation through the courts, especially in the United States. Existing institutional arrangements exist to handle complaints through labour standards enforcement agencies or special tribunals. Job evaluation is relatively common in the public sector and in large organizations. The decentralized system of enterprise-level collective bargaining and wage determination facilitates imposing a comparable worth requirement at the level of the individual enterprise, the level where the comparisons are made under conventional comparable worth.

The labour markets of the European Community are most like those of North America, and in this sense, comparable worth is certainly applicable to those economies. Nevertheless, there is not the same history of anti-discrimination law (especially as it was fostered by the civil rights movement in the United States) and there is not the same tendency towards litigation through the courts. Furthermore, the more centralized bargaining and involvement of labour in determining the social wage provides other mechanisms for achieving the goals of comparable worth without the complex implementation steps. Given the diversity of wage-determining systems that prevail within the EC, there is likely to be a diversity of approaches for attaining the objectives of comparable worth. The best approach will depend upon such factors as: the degree of centralization of wage determination; the extent of unionization or of works councils; the existence of job evaluation procedures; the existence of tribunals or other mechanisms to facilitate individual complaints; differences in the ability to pay comparable worth wage increases; and differences in the extent to which market forces or regulations are acceptable mechanisms for solving social issues.

The application of comparable worth in Japanese-style labour markets is made difficult by a variety of factors: an economic environment that has emphasized efficiency and growth over equity; a legal environment that has not emphasized general anti-discrimination policies, let alone more advanced initiatives like comparable worth; a social environment that emphasizes tradition and the role of women in the home and not in the labour market; a wage-determination system that emphasizes education and seniority over job evaluation; and a complex wage-payment system that involves many components that are not amenable to being incorporated into comparable worth.

In the newly industrialized countries, some differences in the orders of magnitude that may exist (e.g. between men and women in the level and type of education, the importance of physical strength and supervisory responsibility) can be accommodated in comparable worth through the compensable factors of job evaluation, albeit not without difficulty. Other differences that may exist (e.g. the importance of frequent pregnancies and maternity leave, the lack of protective legislation) cannot be so easily accommodated in comparable worth, and hence make its already difficult application even more difficult. Furthermore, there is likely to be considerable resistance to such policies to the extent that they add to the cost of hiring labour and hence may be thought to impede the process of development. Furthermore, the more basic anti-discrimination policies, especially equal employment opportunity policies and education and other policies outside the labour market, are likely to have a stronger role to play in facilitating the integration of women into the process of development.

Developing countries have these implementation problems as well as more severe problems because of the predominance of the informal urban sector and the rural subsistence sector. Comparable worth simply cannot be applied to those sectors given the steps that are required to apply the policy. Furthermore, other policies are likely to have a greater potential impact by facilitating the transition of women from the rural sector and the informal urban sector to the formal urban sector. Such policies include more basic equal pay and equal employment opportunity legislation, as well as initiatives outside of the labour market.

Notes

[1] The Community Charter of Fundamental Social Rights of 1989 is not legally binding, but rather is a "solemn proclamation" to guarantee workers rights in 12 areas. Attempts were made to include the Charter as part of the Maastricht treaty of 1991 which would have provided it with legal status. However, the United Kingdom opposed it, and hence the other 11 members adopted the Charter on a voluntary basis. It does not specifically mention comparable worth, but does include equal treatment for men and women. In most cases, it does not involve new initiatives that are not already in existence in the member countries. Rather, the intent is to ensure a degree of uniformity and harmonization of existing policies.

[2] The role of women, and of anti-discrimination law in Japan, is discussed in the articles by Hayashi and by Hill in Willborn (1991).

[3] Much of the background material for this section and the next section on the developing countries is from Anker and Hein (1985, 1986). Their analysis provides information on such factors as: the extent of employment segregation by sex; determinants of the male-female wage differential; differences in recruiting, hiring, promotion and dismissal practices; and the effect of non-labour market activities, including education and family responsibilities. A variety of methodologies were utilized: theoretical analyses based on alternative perspectives of labour market behaviour; empirical analyses based on international statistics and econometric analyses; case studies of different countries; and extensive interviews of employers and employees. The latter were especially important to provide information on the personnel policies and practices at the level of the individual organization, and to determine the attitudes and reasons that give rise to these practices.

SUMMARY
AND CONCLUDING OBSERVATIONS

13

While there is broad international support for the principle of equal pay for work of equal value, as embodied in ILO Convention No. 100, there is considerable variation in its application on an international basis.

13.1 EARNINGS GAP AND POTENTIAL SCOPE OF COMPARABLE WORTH

Comparable worth is likely to have a much larger potential scope to reduce the earnings gap than conventional equal pay policies, because comparable worth can deal with wage differences that arise because of occupational segregation, while conventional equal pay measures are restricted to comparisons within the same job within the establishment. The potential scope of comparable worth, however, is limited by the fact that comparisons are generally restricted to within the same organization, and hence it cannot deal with the earnings gap that arises because women are disproportionately employed in low wage establishments and industries. Even within establishments its scope is restricted to situations where comparable value can be established. Comparable worth is also unable to deal with the substantial portion of the gap that arises because of differences in productivity-related characteristics like education, training, experience and hours worked, differences that often reflect constraints arising from outside the labour market, especially from household responsibilities.

13.2 DESIGN AND IMPLEMENTATION ISSUES

Numerous technical issues are associated with the design and implementation of comparable worth. These include: definitions of gender dominance; gender bias in job evaluation schemes; pay lines and their appropriate functional form; allowable exemptions (e.g. for merit, seniority, labour shortages); absence of male comparator jobs, especially in all-female establishments; definition of establishment and the employer; opti-

109

mal compliance and enforcement mechanisms (e.g. complaints-based and proactive); phasing and retroactivity; and maximum cost ceilings and time-limits. The design features are particularly important because they can ensure that comparable worth is properly applied, but they can also be manipulated to effectively emasculate the policy. The issue is complicated by the fact that there are not always right or wrong answers in this area. Rather, there are difficult trade-offs among a variety of legitimate competing goals and objectives.

13.3   APPLICATION IN DIFFERENT COUNTRIES

The vast differences in the legal and institutional arrangements that exist across countries in their wage-determination mechanisms suggest that no one single best approach to comparable worth is likely to prevail. Rather than a "one-size-fits-all" approach, different procedures are likely to be necessary, tailored to the particular wage-setting arrangements of the different countries.

Complaints-based procedures do not seem to lead to much activity in the comparable worth area. This may be so because of the usual cost and delays and because the burden of proof usually falls on the complainant, an especially onerous requirement in this area given the complexities involved in the procedure. Allowing unions to instigate the complaint or assist individuals can help in this regard, but unions also come up against obstacles. In most countries that allow enforcement agencies to lodge a complaint, this procedure is seldom applied, especially if the agency also deals with other labour issues. Similarly, labour inspectors, even if they are allowed to instigate a complaint based on their regular inspection process, seldom do so, in part because they have other areas of concern, they are often understaffed, and they may not have the expertise required in this complex area.

Centralized and formalized wage-determination procedures provide a viable mechanism for increasing the wages of females relative to males. However, this is not comparable worth in the conventional sense with its various implementation steps within the establishment. Rather it involves a variety of possible procedures: an overall egalitarian wage policy (e.g. Sweden); elimination of official "markdowns" in female-dominated jobs as in the wage decrees through tribunals (e.g. Australia); and elimination of separate male and female minimum wages in collective agreements or wage awards (e.g. the United Kingdom). Such systems facilitate raising the wages of women because market forces are already blunted, and institutional mechanisms exist to change wages, often by simply eliminating official separate rates.

Proactive policies of comparable worth can also ensure that the policy is implemented as an integral part of the employer's overall compensation system since it is required whether or not a complaint has been made.

However, our experience with such procedures is still limited to a few jurisdictions in Canada and the United States that have adopted such a policy, usually only for their public sector employees. Such proactive systems have their problems, however, not the least of which are the technical and legal issues associated with each stage of implementation.

13.4 EVIDENCE ON THE IMPACT OF COMPARABLE WORTH

In complaints-based systems, only a small portion of the workforce tends to receive adjustments. In proactive, system-wide applications, which have occurred mainly in the public sector in the United States and Canada, larger portions of the workforce receive adjustments although even here there is considerable variation depending upon the proportion of the workforce in female-dominated jobs, and the proportion of those who receive adjustments. When aggregated over a large public sector workforce, perhaps one-third of the workforce may be in female-dominated jobs. However, the proportion of those who receive an adjustment can vary anywhere from around 20 per cent to almost all incumbents of those jobs. It is this variation in "effective coverage" that gives rise to the substantial variation in payroll costs (usually 4 to 8 per cent, but often smaller) even though the wage increase for those who receive an adjustment is often fairly similar, averaging 10 to 20 per cent. The adjustment costs are likely to be substantially smaller (e.g. 1 per cent or less of payroll) in the private sector than in the public sector. This occurs both because smaller portions of the firm's workforce receive an adjustment, and when they do, it tends to be smaller in the private as opposed to the public sector.

In the public sector workforce where these adjustments have been made, they typically raise the ratio of female to male earnings from 0.78 to 0.85 on average, thereby closing about one-third (i.e. 0.07/0.22) of the overall male-female wage gap within the organization. The remaining gap reflects a variety of factors: differences in job evaluation points; a lack of male comparators; males in female-dominated jobs who receive an adjustment; and women employed in mixed or male-dominated jobs who do not receive an adjustment.

Simulation results for the American economy as a whole suggest that an economy-wide application of comparable worth would close 8 to 20 per cent of the wage gap. The majority of the wage gap would not be closed, reflecting differences in the skill, effort, responsibility and working conditions between male- and female-dominated jobs, as well as the fact that many women are employed in mixed or male-dominated jobs. Moreover, the overall gap in the economy as a whole reflects differences in pay across establishments and industries, neither of which are within the scope of conventional comparable worth procedures.

There is considerable controversy about the employment impacts of comparable worth. Most studies suggest that the adverse employment effect would be small because employers would not substantially reduce their employment growth in jobs that received the wage increases, in spite of the fact that the wage increases are fairly substantial. Some studies, however, find the adverse employment effect to be small simply because the independent impact of comparable worth on wages is calculated to be small. Others find moderate impacts on both wages and employment growth. In all cases, however, any adverse employment effect occurs in the form of slower employment growth rather than in the form of absolute employment reductions, since overall employment growth has tended to be substantial for women.

13.5   APPLICATION IN DIFFERENT ECONOMIC SYSTEMS

In the market-oriented systems of the United States and Canada, where comparable worth has been most extensively applied, a number of conditions prevail that facilitate its application: considerable experience with anti-discrimination law and litigation through the courts; existing institutional arrangements exist to handle complaints through labour standards enforcement agencies or special tribunals; job evaluation in the public sector and in large organizations; and a decentralized system of enterprise-level collective bargaining and wage determination which facilitates imposing a comparable worth requirement at the level of the individual enterprise where the comparisons are made under conventional comparable worth.

The labour markets of the European Community are most like those of the United States and Canada and, in this sense, comparable worth is certainly applicable to those economies. Nevertheless, there is not the same history of anti-discrimination law nor the same tendency towards litigation through the courts. Furthermore, the more centralized bargaining and involvement of labour in determining the social wage provides other mechanisms for achieving the goals of comparable worth without the complex implementation steps. Given the diversity of wage determining systems that prevail within the EC, there is likely to be a diversity of approaches for attaining the objectives of comparable worth. The best approach will depend upon such factors as: the degree of centralization of wage determination; the extent of unionization or of works councils; the existence of job evaluation procedures; the existence of tribunals or other mechanisms to facilitate individual complaints; differences in the ability to pay comparable worth wage increases; and differences in the extent to which market forces or regulation are acceptable mechanisms for solving social issues.

The application of comparable worth in Japanese-style labour markets is made difficult by a variety of factors: an economic environment that has emphasized efficiency and growth over equity; a legal environment that has not emphasized general anti-discrimination policies, let alone more advanced initiatives like comparable worth; a social environment that emphasizes tradition and the role of women in the home and not in the labour market; a wage-determination system that emphasizes education and seniority over job evaluation; and a complex wage payment system that involves many components that are not amenable to being incorporated into comparable worth.

In the newly industrializing countries, some differences (e.g. between men and women in the level and type of education, the importance of physical strength and supervisory responsibility) can be accommodated in comparable worth through the compensable factors of job evaluation, albeit not without difficulty. Other differences (e.g. the importance of absenteeism, turnover, maternity leave, protective legislation) cannot be so easily accommodated in comparable worth, and hence make its already difficult application even more difficult. Furthermore, there is likely to be considerable resistance to such policies to the extent that they add cost and hence impede the process of development. Additionally, the more basic anti-discrimination policies, especially equal employment opportunity policies and education and other policies outside the labour market, are likely to have a stronger role to play to facilitate the integration of women into the process of development.

Developing countries have these implementation problems as well as more severe problems because of the predominance of the informal urban sector and the rural subsistence sector where comparable worth simply cannot be applied. Furthermore, other policies are likely to have a greater potential impact by facilitating the transition of women from the rural sector and the informal urban sector to the formal urban sector. Such policies include the more basic equal pay and equal employment opportunity legislation, as well as facilitating initiatives outside the labour market.

Clearly, comparable worth is not a policy that has uniform applicability to different economic systems, in spite of the fact that all have a "comparable worth wage gap". When the policy itself is applied, it should be adapted to the particular wage-determination processes of each system. Furthermore, an examination should be made of alternative policies that can be used to achieve the same goals of comparable worth, perhaps in a more effective fashion, without the complexity of the conventional comparable worth implementation process. The variety of approaches will also provide information on the pros and cons of the different approaches for achieving the goals of the complex and relatively new policy.

13.6   CONCLUDING OBSERVATIONS

Comparable worth is a complex policy instrument in spite of the fact that the principle of equal pay for work of equal value seems like a simple concept. Translating this simple theoretical principle into a practical policy that can be implemented in an effective fashion, however, is not a straightforward matter.

Comparable worth has been interpreted and implemented in various ways in different countries. To a large degree this is appropriate, since different countries have their own institutional arrangements and labour market mechanisms that can facilitate or hinder the implementation of the policy. Moreover, they may have alternative ways of achieving the same objectives in a more effective fashion and with fewer implementation complexities.

Throughout the text, references have been made to areas where more research and information is needed on this important policy. At the theoretical level, there is still room for debate about the appropriateness of the concept of value that is embodied in comparable worth. That concept should be contrasted not with an economic concept of value in an *abstract* sense where markets work perfectly, but rather with a *realistic* comparison of comparable worth where market outcomes are influenced by discrimination emanating from both the labour market and from outside the labour market. In an imperfect world, comparisons invariably involve imperfect alternatives. In essence, even if the concept of value involved in comparable worth is a flawed concept, the issue is whether it can still be an effective policy instrument for reducing the discriminatory portion of the male-female earnings gap. Of course, such a decision requires a comparison of the pros and cons of other policies for achieving the same objectives, as well as other legitimate objectives such as the reduction of poverty or income inequality.

At the practical level, there are a myriad of technical, design and implementation issues that are in need of more analysis to ensure that comparable worth is administered in an effective fashion to achieve its objectives with a minimum of adverse consequences. As indicated, it is important to do this in advance and independent of particular applications so that decisions can be made on the basis of the appropriate procedure, rather than on the basis of its particular effect in a specific application.

At the empirical level, more information is needed on a variety of dimensions. At the aggregate level, it would be informative to know what is happening to the male-female earnings gap across different countries, after controlling for changes in the productivity-related factors that may be occurring, especially associated with the changing composition of the female workforce. At the aggregate level, it would also be informative to have more evidence on how the overall earnings gap is affected by the different policies that have been applied in different countries.

At the micro level, in cases where comparable worth has been applied, it would be informative to have more information on a variety of factors: the effect of the different implementation practices; the determinants of the variation in the proportion of persons who receive an award and the magnitude of the award; the long-term effect on wages and employment; the impact on wage structures, hiring practices, subcontracting, morale, productivity, turnover, fringe benefits, occupational segregation and collective bargaining; and the effect on the private sector as opposed to the public sector.

Clearly, information on any or all of these factors would be useful to determine the impact of comparable worth and how it can be applied in a more effective fashion in different economic systems. One of the side benefits of the variation in the application of the policy on an international basis is that there is a diversity of experience that can be evaluated. Such diversity should provide information on the pros and cons of the different implementation procedures. This, in turn, should facilitate learning from the mistakes of others and adopting "best practices" in this important area.

An international perspective is increasingly important on all policy issues, given the growing internationalization and interdependence of economies that prevails. It is especially important for policies such as comparable worth, however, given its complexity and the fact that it is a relatively new policy. We have much to learn, and the diversity of international experience provides us with a laboratory from which to learn.

BIBLIOGRAPHY

Aaron, Henry J.; Cameran, M. Lougy. 1986. *The comparable worth controversy* (Washington, DC, Brookings Institution).

Abbott, Mike. 1989. "Equal value tests for pay equity", in R. Chaykowski (ed.): *Pay equity legislation: Linking economic issues and policy concerns* (Kingston, Ontario, Queen's University, Industrial Relations Centre), pp. 20-35.

Acker, Joan. 1987. "Sex bias in job evaluation: A comparable worth issue", in Christine Bose; Glenna Spitze (eds.): *Ingredients for women's employment policy* (Albany, New York, State University of New York Press).

–. 1989. *Doing comparable worth: Gender, class and pay equity* (Philadelphia, Temple University Press).

Ad Hoc Working Group on Equal Pay and Job Classification Systems. 1981. *Industrial discrimination by the use of job classification systems* (Brussels, Commission of the European Community).

Aldrich, Mark; and Buchele, Robert. 1986. *The economics of comparable worth* (Cambridge, Massachusetts, Ballinger).

Ames, Lynda. 1991. "Legislating equity: A comparison of provincial legislation in Manitoba and Ontario requiring pay equity", in *International Journal of Public Administration*, Vol. 14, Winter, pp. 871-892.

Anker, Richard; Hein, Catherine. 1985. "Why Third World urban employers usually prefer men", *International Labour Review* (Geneva, ILO), Vol. 124, Jan.-Feb., pp. 73-90.

–; –. 1986. *Sex inequalities in urban employment in the Third World* (London, Macmillan).

Arrowsmith, David. 1986. *Pay equity: Legislative framework and cases* (Kingston, Ontario, Industrial Relations Centre, Queen's University).

Arthurs, A. 1988. "Job evaluation: The impact of equal value", in *Equal Opportunities International*, Vol. 7, No. 6, pp. 3-5.

Arvey, Richard D. 1986. "Sex bias in job evaluation procedures", in *Personnel Psychology*, Vol. 39, Summer, pp. 315-335.

Arvey, Richard D.; Holt, Katherine. 1988. "The cost of alternative comparable worth strategies", in *Compensation and Benefits Review*, Vol. 20, Sep.-Oct., pp. 37-46.

Arvey, Richard D. et al. 1985. "Reliability artifacts in comparable worth procedures", in *Journal of Applied Psychology*, Vol. 70, pp. 695-705.

Atkins, S. 1983. "Equal pay for work of equal value", in *Public Law*, Spring, pp. 19-29.

Avebury Research & Consulting Ltd. 1991. *What works ... experiences with implementation of the pay equity legislation: Final report*, 2 vols. (Toronto, Canadian Facts).

Beider, Perry C. et al. 1988. "Comparable worth in a general equilibrium model of the US economy" in Ronald G. Ehrenberg (ed.): *Research in Labor Economics*, Vol. 9 (Greenwich, Connecticut, JAI Press).

Bellace, Janice R. 1980. "A foreign perspective", in E. Robert Livernash (ed.), *Comparable worth issues and alternatives* (Washington, DC, Equal Employment Advisory Council).

–. 1984. "Comparable worth: Proving sex-based wage discrimination", in *Iowa Law Review*, Vol. 69, March, pp. 655-704.

–. 1987. "The impact of the American and British equal pay guarantee on job evaluation", in *Applied Psychology: An International Review*, Vol. 36, pp. 9-24.

Bennett, Laura. 1988. "Equal pay and comparable worth and the Australian Conciliation and Arbitration Commission", in *Journal of Industrial Relations*, Vol. 30, Dec., pp. 533-545.

Bennett, Shirley Leh. 1988. "Comparable worth: The sex and salary debate", in *Nursing and Health Care*, Vol. 9, May, pp. 245-247.

Bergmann, Barbara R. 1988. *The economic emergence of women* (New York, Basic Books).

–. 1987. "Pay equity — surprising answers to hard questions", in *Challenge*, May-June, pp. 45-51.

Blau, F. D.; Beller, A. H. 1988. "Trends in earnings differential by gender, 1971-1981", in *Industrial and Labor Relations Review*, Vol. 41, July, pp. 513-529.

Blau, Francine; Ferber, Marianne. 1987. "Discrimination: Empirical evidence from the United States", in *American Economic Review*, Vol. 77, May, pp. 316-320.

Blau, F.; Kahn, L.. 1992. "The gender earnings gap: Learning from international comparisons", in *American Economic Review*, Vol. 82, May, pp. 533-538.

Blumrosen, Ruth G. 1986. "Remedies for wage discrimination", in *University of Michigan Journal of Law Reform*, Vol. 20, pp. 99-161.

Bonnell, Sheila M. 1987. "The effect of equal pay for females on the composition of employment in Australia", in *Economic Record*, Vol. 63, pp. 340-351.

Booker, Sharon; Nuckolls, L. Camille. 1986. "Legal and economic aspects of comparable worth", in *Public Personnel Management*, Vol. 15, Summer, pp. 189-206.

Buchele, R.; Aldrich, M. 1985. "How much difference would comparable worth make?", in *Industrial Relations*, Vol. 24, Spring, pp. 222-233.

Burton, Clare et al. 1987. *Women's worth: Pay equity and job evaluation in Australia* (Canberra, Australian Government Publishing Service).

Cain, Glen. 1986. "The economic analysis of labour market discrimination: A survey", in Orley Ashenfelter; Richard Layard (eds.), *Handbook of labour economics*, Vol. 1 (Amsterdam, Elsevier Science Publishers), pp. 693-785.

Canadian Facts. 1992. *Outcomes of pay equity for organizations employing 100 to 499 employees in Ontario* (Toronto, Pay Equity Office).

Chaykowski, Richard (ed.). 1990. *Pay equity legislation: Linking economic issues and policy concerns* (Kingston, Ontario, Queen's University, Industrial Relations Centre).

Chiplin, Brian et al. 1980. "Relative female earnings in Great Britain and impact of legislation", in Peter Sloane (ed.), *Women and low pay* (London, Macmillan), pp. 57-126.

Cihon, Patrick. 1988. "Comparable worth: The Quebec experience", in *Journal of Collective Negotiations in the Public Sector*, Vol. 17, No. 3, pp. 249-255.

Cihon, P.; Wesman, E. 1988. "Comparable worth: The U.S./Canadian experience", in *Loyola Los Angeles International and Comparative Law Journal*, Vol. 10, No. 1, pp. 57-107.

Clauss, Carin A. 1986. "Comparable worth — the theory, its legal foundation, and the feasibility of implementation", in *University of Michigan Journal of Law Reform*, Vol. 20, pp. 7-97.

Commission on the Economic Status of Women, State of Minnesota. 1985. *Newsletter No. 104* (St. Paul, Minnesota, Commission on the Economic Status of Women).

Conklin, David; Bergman, Paul (eds.). 1990. *Pay equity in Ontario: A manager's guide* (Halifax, Nova Scotia, Institute for Research on Public Policy).

Conway, Heather E. 1987. *Equal pay for work of equal value legislation in Canada: An analysis* (Ottawa, Institute for Research on Public Policy).

Cook, Alice. 1985. *Comparable worth: A case book of experiences in states and localities* (University of Hawaii at Manoa, Industrial Relations Center).

–. 1986. *Comparable worth: A case book of experiences in states and localities. 1986 supplement* (University of Hawaii at Manoa, Industrial Relations Center).

Craig, Christine. 1977. "Towards national job evaluation? Trends and attitudes in Britain and in the Netherlands", in *Industrial Relations Journal*, Vol. 8, Spring, p. 30.

Day, Tannis. 1987. *Pay equity: Some issues in the debate* (Ottawa, Canadian Advisory Council on the Status of Women).

Drago, R. 1989. "The extent of wage discriminatiion in Australia", *Australian Bulletin of Labour*, Vol. 15, No. 4, pp. 313-325.

Duplessis-Novitz, R.; Jaber, N.. 1990. "Pay equity, the 'free' market and state intervention", in *New Zealand Journal of Industrial Relations*, Vol. 15, No. 3, pp. 251-262.

Edwards, L. N. 1988. "Equal employment opportunity in Japan: A view from the West", in *Industrial and Labor Relations Review*, Vol. 41, Jan., pp. 240-250.

Egri, Carolyn; Stanbury, W. T. 1989. "How pay equity legislation came to Ontario", in *Canadian Public Administration*, Vol. 32, Summer, pp. 274-303.

Ehrenberg, Ronald G.; Smith, Robert S. 1987. "Comparable-worth wage adjustments and female employment in the state and local sector", in *Journal of Labor Economics*, Vol. 5, pp. 43-62.

Elizur, Dov. 1987. *Systematic job evaluation and comparable worth* (Aldershot, Hampshire, Gower).

Elliott, Cheryl; Saxe, Stewart. 1987. *Pay equity handbook: A step-by-step guide to implementing equal pay for work of equal value in Ontario* (Aurora, Ontario, Canada Law Book).

England, Paula; Norris, Bahar. 1985. "Comparable worth: A new doctrine of sex discrimination", in *Social Science Quarterly*, Vol. 66, pp. 629-643.

Ephron, Susan. 1986. "The equal pay guarantee in the EEC", in *Cooperative Labor Law*, Vol. 7, Winter, pp. 197-209.

Evans, Sara M.; Nelson, Barbara J. 1986. "Initiating a comparable worth wage policy in Minnesota: Notes from the field", in *Policy Studies Review*, Vol. 5, pp. 849-862.

–; –. 1989. *Wage justice: Comparable worth and the paradox of technocratic reform* (Chicago, University of Chicago Press).

Eyraud, F. et al. 1992. *Equal pay protection in industrialized market economies: In search of greater effectiveness* (Geneva, International Labour Office).

Feldberg, R.L. 1984. "Comparable worth: Toward theory and practice in the United States", in *Signs*, Vol. 10, Winter, pp. 311-328.

Ferber, Marianne. 1991. "Women in the labor market", in *International Review of Comparative Public Policy* , Vol. 3, pp. 39-60.

Fischel, Daniel R.; Lazear, Edward P. 1986. "Comparable worth and discrimination in labor markets", in *University of Chicago Law Review*, Vol. 53, pp. 891-918.

Flam, Harry. 1987. "Equal pay for unequal work", in *Scandinavian Journal of Economics*, Vol. 89, No. 4, pp. 435-450.

Flammang, Janet A. 1986. "Effective implementation: The case of comparable worth in San Jose", in *Policy Studies Review*, Vol. 5, May, pp. 815-837.

Flanagan, Thomas. 1987a. "Equal pay for work of equal value: An historical note", *Journal of Canadian Studies*, Vol. 22, Fall, pp. 5-19.

–. 1987b. "Equal pay for work of equal value: Some theoretical criticisms", *Canadian Public Policy*, Vol. 13, Dec. pp. 435-444.

Freed, Mayer G.; Polsby, Daniel D. 1984. "Comparable worth in the Equal Pay Act", in *University of Chicago Law Review*, Vol. 51, pp. 1078-1111.

Freeman, E. 1987. "Community law (EEC) and work of equal value", in *Cambridge Law Journal*, Vol. 46, Nov., pp. 410-412.

Fudge, Judy. 1991. "Limiting equity: The definition of 'employer' under the Ontario Pay Equity Act", in *Canadian Journal of Women and the Law*, Vol. 4, No. 2, pp. 556-563.

Fudge, Judy; McDermott, Pat (eds.). 1991. *Just wages: A feminist assessment of pay equity* (Toronto, University of Toronto Press).

Gethman, Barton R. 1987. "The job market, sex bias, and comparable worth", in *Public Personnel Management*, Vol. 16, Summer, pp. 173-180.

Gold, Michael. 1983. *A dialogue on comparable worth* (Ithaca, New York, ILR Press).

Goodwin, Cynthia. 1984. *Equal pay legislation and implementation: Selected countries* (Ottawa, Labour Canada).

Grams, Robert; Schwab, Donald. 1985. "An investigation of systematic gender-related error in job evaluation", in *Academy of Management Journal*, Vol. 28, June, pp. 279-290.

Greenwood, Daphne. 1984. "The institutional inadequacy of the market in determining comparable worth: Implications for value theory", in *Journal of Economic Issues*, Vol. 18, June, pp. 457-464.

Gregory, R. G. et al. 1989. "Women's pay in Australia, Great Britain and the United States: The role of laws, regulations and human capital", in R. T. Michael et al. (eds.), *Pay equity empirical inquiries* (Washington, DC, National Academy Press).

Gregory, R. G.; Daly, A. 1991. "Can economic theory explain why Australian women are so well paid relative to their United States counterparts?", in *International Review of Comparative Public Policy*, Vol. 3, pp. 81-128.

Gregory, R. G.; Duncan, R. C. 1981. "Segmented labor market theories and the Australian experience of equal pay for women", in *Journal of Post Keynesian Economics*, Vol. 2, Spring, pp. 403-428.

–; –. 1983. "Equal pay for women: A reply", in *Australia Economic Papers*, Vol. 22, June, pp. 60-67.

Gunderson, Morley. 1975. "Male-female wage differentials and the impact of equal pay legislation", in *Review of Economic Statistics*, Vol. 57, Nov., pp. 462-469.

–. 1985. "Spline function estimates of the impact of equal pay legislation: The Ontario experience", in *Relations Industrielles*, Vol. 40, pp. 775-791.

–. 1989a. "Male-female wage differentials and policy responses", in *Journal of Economic Literature*, Vol. 27, March, pp. 46-72.

–. 1989b. "Implementation of comparable worth in Canada", in *Journal of Social Issues*, Vol. 45, Winter, pp. 209-222.

Gunderson, Morley; Riddell, W. Craig. 1988. *Labour market economics: Theory, evidence and policy in Canada* (Toronto, McGraw-Hill Ryerson).

–; –. 1991. "Economics of women's wages in Canada", in *International Review of Comparative Public Policy*, Vol. 3, pp. 151-178.

–; –. 1992. "Comparable worth: Canada's experience", in *Contemporary Policy Issues*, Vol. 10, July 1992, pp. 85-94.

Gunderson, Morley; Robb, Roberta Edgecombe. 1991a. "Equal pay for work of equal value: Canada's experience", in *Advances in Industrial and Labour Relations*, Vol. 5, pp. 151-168.

–; –. 1991b. "Legal and institutional issues pertaining to women's wages in Canada", in *International Review of Comparative Public Policy*, Vol. 3, pp. 129-150.

Hartmann, Heidi (ed.). 1985. *Comparable worth: New directions for research* (Washington, DC, National Academy Press).

Hartmann, Heidi; O'Neill, June. 1985. "Comparable worth controversy", in *New Perspectives*, Vol. 17, Spring, pp. 28-33.

Hayashi, H. 1991. "Issues in Japan on the wages of women workers", in *International Review of Comparative Public Policy*, Vol. 3, pp. 243-260.

Hill, M. Anne. 1991. "Women's relative wages in postwar Japan", in *International Review of Comparative Public Policy*, Vol. 3, pp. 261-288.

Hill, M. Anne; Killingsworth, Mark (eds.). 1989. *Comparable worth: Analyses and evidence* (Ithaca, New York, ILR Press).

Hoffman, Carl C.; Hoffman, Kathleen P. 1987. "Does comparable worth obscure the real issues?", in *Personnel Journal*, Vol. 66, Jan., pp. 83-95.

Holzhauer, James D. 1986. "The economic possibilities of comparable worth", in *University of Chicago Law Review*, Vol. 53, pp. 919-933.

Horrell, S. et al. 1989. "Unequal jobs or unequal pay?", in *Industrial Relations Journal*, Vol. 20, No. 3, pp. 176-191.

Horrigan, June; Harriman, Ann. 1988. "Comparable worth: Public sector unions and employers provide a model for implementing pay equity", in *Labour Law Review*, Vol. 39, Oct., pp. 704-711.

Hutner, Frances C. 1986. *Equal pay for comparable worth: The working woman's issue of the eighties* (New York, Praeger).

Hyman, Prue. 1988. "Equal pay for work of equal value — job evaluation issues", in *New Zealand Journal of Industrial Relations*, Vol. 13, Dec., pp. 237-255.

ILO. 1986. *General survey of the reports on the equal remuneration convention (No. 100) and remuneration (No. 90), 1951* (Geneva, International Labour Office).

–. 1992. *Report of the Committee of Experts on the Application of Conventions and Recommendations*, Report III (Part 4A), International Labour Conference, 79th Session (Geneva, 1992).

Jaussaud, Danielle. 1984. "Can job evaluation systems help determine the comparable worth of male and female occupations?", in *Journal of Economic Issues*, Vol. 18, June, pp. 473-482.

Jefferson, M. 1985. "Equal pay for work of equal value: A comment on Hayward v. Cammell Laird", in *Industrial Relations Journal*, Vol. 16, Summer, pp. 76-80.

–. 1990. "The effects of equal value claims on businesses", in *Industrial Relations Journal*, Vol. 21, No. 1, pp. 7-13.

Johansen, Elaine. 1984a. *Comparable worth: The myth and the movement* (Boulder, Colorado, Westview Press).

–. 1984b. "Managing the revolution: The case for comparable worth", in *Review of Public Personnel Administration*, Vol. 4, Spring, pp. 14-27.

–. 1984c. "From social doctrine to implementation: Agenda setting in comparable worth", in *Policy Studies Review*, Vol. 4, Aug., pp. 71-85.

–. 1985. "Comparable worth: The character of a controversy", in *Public Administration Review*, Vol. 45, Sep.-Oct., pp. 631-635.

Johnson, George; Solon, Gary. 1986. "Estimates of the direct effects of comparable worth policy", in *American Economic Review*, Vol. 76, Dec., pp. 117-125.

Juriansz, R. G. 1987a. "Anti-discrimination law", in *Ottawa Law Review*, Vol. 19, No. 2, pp. 447-511.

–. 1987b. "Anti-discrimination law, part II", in *Ottawa Law Review*, Vol. 19, No. 3, pp. 667-721.

Kahn, Shulamit. 1992. "Economic implications of public-sector comparable worth: The case of San Jose, California", in *Industrial Relations*, Vol. 31, Spring, pp. 270-289.

Katz, Marsha et al. 1986. "Comparable worth: Analysis of cases and implications for H. R. management", in *Compensation and Benefits Review*, Vol. 18, May-June, pp. 26-38.

Kelly, John G. 1988. *Pay equity management* (Don Mills, Ontario, CCH Canadian Ltd.).

Kelly, Rita; Jane Bayes (eds.). 1988. *Comparable worth, pay equity, and public policy* (New York, Greenwood Press).

Kilberg, W. J. 1985. "The earnings gap and comparable worth", in *Employee Relations Law Journal*, Vol. 10, Spring, pp. 579-583.

Killingsworth, Mark R. 1985. "Comparable worth in the job market: Estimating its effect", in *Monthly Labor Review*, Vol. 108, July, pp. 39-41.

–. 1987. "Heterogeneous preferences, compensating wage differentials and comparable worth", in *Quarterly Journal of Economics*, Vol. 102, pp. 727-742.

–. 1990. *The economics of comparable worth* (Kalamazoo, Michigan, W.E. Upjohn).

Kramar, R.; Plowman, D. H. 1991. "The quest for parity: Legal initiatives and women's wages in Australia", in *International Review of Comparative Public Policy*, Vol. 3, pp. 63-80.

Landau, C. E. 1984. "Recent legislation and case law in the EEC on sex equality in employment", in *International Labour Review*, Vol. 123, Jan.-Feb, pp. 53-70.

Landau, Eve. 1992. "International labour standards: The case of equal pay-European perspective", in Alan Gladstone et al. (eds.), *Labour Relations in a Changing Environment* (Berlin, Walter de Gruyter).

Lester, A.; Rose, D. 1991. "Equal value claims and sex bias in collective bargaining", in *Industrial Law Journal*, Vol. 20, No. 3, pp. 163-175.

Levine, Marvin J. 1987. "Comparable worth in the 1980's: Will collective bargaining supplant legislative initiatives and judicial interpretations?", in *Labor Law Journal*, Vol. 38, June, pp. 323-334.

Livernash, E. Robert (ed.). 1984. *Comparable worth: Issues and alternatives* (Washington, DC, Equal Employment Advisory Council).

Lloyd, Cynthia; Neimi, Beth. 1979. *The economics of sex differentials* (New York City, New York, Columbia University Press).

Lowe, Rosemary; Wittig, Michele. 1989. "Approaching pay equity through comparable worth", in *"Journal of Social Issues*, Vol. 45 No. 4.

Lupica, Lois R. 1988. "Pay equity – a 'cockamamie idea'? The future of health care may depend upon it", in *American Journal of Law and Medicine*, Vol.13, Winter, pp. 597-620.

Mackenzie, M. Elizabeth. 1988. *The Ontario Pay Equity Act and its effect on collective bargaining* (Kingston, Ontario, Queen's University School of Business).

Madden, J. "The persistence of pay differentials: The economics of sex discrimination", in *Women and Work*, Vol. 1 (Beverly Hills, Ca., Sage Publishing, 1985).

Madigan, R. M.; Hoover, D. J.. 1986. "Effects of alternative job evaluation methods on decisions involving pay equity", in *Academy of Management Journal*, Vol. 29, pp. 84-100.

Mahoney, Thomas A. 1987. "Understanding comparable worth: A societal and political perspective", in *Research in Organizational Behavior*, Vol. 9, pp. 209-245.

Mahoney, T. A. et al. 1984. "Where do compensation specialists stand on comparable worth?", in *Compensation Review*, Vol. 16, No. 4, pp. 27-40.

Mangum, Stephen L. 1988a. "Comparable worth and pay setting in the public and private sectors", in *Journal of Collective Negotiations in the Public Sector*, Vol. 17, No. 1, pp. 1-12.

–. 1988b. "The male-female comparable worth debate: alternative economic perspectives on an issue that cuts across the social sciences", in *American Journal of Economics and Sociology*, Vol. 47, April, pp. 149-165.

Manitoba, Civil Service Commission. 1988. *Pay Equity Implementation in the Manitoba Civil Service* (Winnipeg, Manitoba Civil Service Commission).

Marcotte, Marilee. 1987. *Equal pay for work of equal value* (Kingston, Ontario, Queen's University, Industrial Relations Centre).

McArthur, L. Z.; Obrant, S. W. 1986. "Sex biases in comparable worth analyses", in *Journal of Applied Social Psychology*, Vol. 16, pp. 757-770.

McCrudden, Christopher. 1983. "Equal pay for work of equal value: The equal pay (amendment) regulations 1983", in *Industrial Law Journal*, Vol. 12, Dec., pp. 197-219.

–. 1984. "Equal pay for work of equal value", in *Industrial Law Journal*, Vol. 13, No. 1, March.

–. 1986. "Comparable worth: A common dilemma", in *Yale Journal of International Law*, Vol. 11, Spring, pp. 396-436.

–. 1987. *Women, employment and European equality law* (London, Eclipse).

–. 1991. "Between legality and reality: Implementation of equal pay for work of equal value in Great Britain", in *International Review of Comparative Public Policy*, Vol. 3, pp. 179-220

McDermott, Patricia. 1990. "Pay equity in Ontario: A critical legal analysis", in *Osgoode Hall Law Journal*, Vol. 28, Summer, pp. 381-407.

–. 1991. "Pay equity in Canada", in Judy Fudge; Patricia McDermott (eds.), *Just wages: A feminist assessment of pay equity* (Toronto, University of Toronto Press).

McNally, Joyce; Shimmin, Sylvia. 1984. "Job evaluation and equal pay for work of equal value", in *Personnel Review*, Vol. 13, No. 1, pp. 27-31.

McGavin, P. A. 1983. "Equal pay for women: A re-assessment of the Australian experience", in *Australian Economic Papers*, Vol. 22, June, pp. 48-59.

Mead, Geoffrey. 1988. "Equal pay and EEC law", in *Industrial Law Journal*, Vol. 17, Dec., pp. 244-248.

Michael, Robert T. et al. (eds.). 1989. *Pay equity: Empirical inquiries* (Washington, DC, National Academy Press).

Mincer, Jacob. 1985. "Intercountry comparisons of labor force trends and of related developments: An overview", in *Journal of Labor Economics*, Vol. 3, Jan., pp. S1-S32.

Moore, R. L. 1987. "Are male-female earnings differentials related to life-expectancy-caused pension cost differences?", in *Economic Inquiry*, Vol. 25, July, pp. 385-401.

Mori, Masumi. 1992. "Evaluating the effectiveness of the equal opportunity law", in *Economic Eye*, Winter, pp. 8-17.

Mount, Michael; Ellis, Rebecca. 1987. "Investigation of bias in job evaluation ratings of comparable worth study participants", in *Personnel Psychology*, Vol. 40, Spring, pp. 85-96.

Moyers, Gene. 1985. "The comparable worth debate: The equal rights issue of the 80s", in *Public Management*, Vol. 67, Aug., pp. 2-4.

Mulcahy, Robert W.; Anderson, Jon E. 1986. "Comparable worth", in *Public Personnel Management*, Vol. 15, Fall, pp. 233-247.

Nakamura, Alice; Nakamura, Masao. 1989. "Effects of comparable worth programs", in *Journal of Social Issues*, Vol. 45, No. 4, pp. 191-208.

National Committee on Pay Equity. 1990. *Legislating pay equity to raise women's wages: A progress report on the implementation of the Ontario, Canada Pay Equity Act* (Washington, DC, The Committee).

—. 1989. *Pay equity in the public sector, 1979-1989* (Washington, DC, The Committee).

O'Donovan, Katherine; Szyszczak, Erika. 1988. *Equality and sex discrimination law* (Oxford, Blackwell).

O'Neill, June. 1985. "The trend in the male-female wage gap in the United States", in *Journal of Labor Economics*, Vol. 3, Jan., pp. S91-S116.

O'Neill, June et al. 1989. "Effects of comparable worth policy: Evidence from Washington State", in *American Economic Review*, Vol. 79, May, pp. 305-309.

Oi, Walter Y. 1986. "Neglected women and other implications of comparable worth", in *Contemporary Policy Issues*, Vol. 4, Apr., pp. 21-32.

Ontario, Consultation Panel on Pay Equity. 1986. *Report of the Consultation Panel on Pay Equity* (Toronto, Ontario Women's Directorate).

Ontario, Minister Responsible for Women's Issues. 1985. *Green Paper on pay equity* (Toronto, The Minister).

Ontario, Ministry of Labour. 1990. *Policy Directions Amending the Pay Equity Act.* March.

—. 1991. *Extending pay equity by proportional value and proxy comparisons* (Toronto, Ontario Ministry of Labour).

Ontario, Pay Equity Commission. 1989. *Report to the Minister on the Options Relating to the Achievement of Pay Equity in Sectors of the Economy Which are Predominantly Female* (Toronto, Pay Equity Commission).

—. 1991. *Annual Report, 1989-90* (Toronto, Pay Equity Commission).

Orazem, P.; Mattila, J. P. 1990. "The implementation process of comparable worth: Winners and losers", in *Journal of Political Economy*, Feb., pp. 134-152.

Organization for Economic Co-operation and Development. 1991a. *Employment outlook* (Paris, OECD).

—. 1991b. *Equal pay for work of comparable worth: The experience of industrialised countries* (Paris, OECD).

Palmer, Ingrid. 1991. *Gender and population in the adjustment of African economies: Planning for change* (Geneva, International Labour Office).

Patten, Thomas. 1988. *Fair pay: The managerial challenge of comparable job worth and job evaluation* (San Francisco, Jossey-Bass).

Pesando, James et al. 1991. "Pension benefits and male-female wage differentials", in *Canadian Journal of Economics*, Vol. 24, August, pp. 536-550.

Pfeffer, Jeffrey; Davis-Blake, Alison. 1987. "The effect of the proportion of women on salaries: The case of college administrators", in *Administrative Science Quarterly*, Vol. 32, March, pp. 1-24.

Pierson, D. et al. 1984. "A policy capturing application in a union setting", in H. Remick (ed.), *Comparable worth and wage discrimination* (Philadelphia, Temple University Press).

Provis, Chris. 1986. "Comparative wage justice", in *Journal of Industrial Relations*, Vol. 28, No. 1, pp. 24-39.

Rafferty, Felicity. 1989. "Equal pay — past experience, future directions: A practioner's perspective", in *Journal of Industrial Relations*, Vol. 31, No. 4, pp. 526-537.

–. 1991. "Pay equity: An industrial relations anomaly?", in *Journal of Industrial Relations*, Vol. 33, pp. 3-19.

Raisian, John et al. 1988. "Implementing comparable worth: Conceptual issues and impacts", in Garth Mangum; Peter Philips (eds.), *Three worlds of labor economics* (Armonk, New York, M. E. Sharpe, Inc.), pp. 183-200.

Reichenberg, Neil E. 1986. "Pay equity in review", in *Public Personnel Management*, Vol. 15, Fall, pp. 211-232.

Richbell, Suzanne. 1988. "Equal value through job evaluation: Perspectives on recent British experience", in *Equal Opportunities International*, Vol. 7, No. 2, pp. 311-315.

Remick, Helen (ed.). 1984. *Comparable worth and wage discrimination* (Philadelphia, Temple University Press).

Robb, Roberta. 1987. "Equal pay for work of equal value: Issues and policies", in *Canadian Public Policy*, Vol. 13, Dec., pp. 445-461.

Robb, Barrie G. 1988. *The Pay Equity Act of Ontario: Implications for collective bargaining* (Kingston, Ontario, Queen's University).

Romanoff, Kent et al. 1986. "Pay equity: Internal and external consideration", in *Compensation and Benefits Review*, Vol. 18, May-June, pp. 17-25.

Rubery, Jill, 1992. *The economics of equal value*, in Research Discussion Series No. 3 (Equal Opportunity Commission, Manchester).

Rubinstein, Michael. 1984. *Equal pay for work of equal value: The new regulations and their implications* (London, Macmillan Press).

–. 1986. "Discriminatory job evaluation and the law", *Comparative Labour Law*, Vol. 7, Winter, pp. 172-195.

–. 1988. *Discrimination: A guide to the relevant case law on race and sex discrimination and equal pay* (1st ed.) (London, Eclipse).

Schlafly, P. 1985. "Shall I compare thee to a plumber's pay? Comparable worth collapses", in *Policy Review*, Vol. 31, Winter, pp. 76-78.

Schmid, Gunther; Weitzel, Renate. 1984. *Sex discrimination and equal opportunity* (Berlin, WZB Publications).

Schneibal, William. 1988. "The continued viability of Title VII comparable worth actions", in *Public Personnel Management*, Vol. 17, Fall, pp. 315-322.

Schofield, Peter. 1988. "Permitted comparisons", in *Industrial Law Journal*, Vol. 17, Dec., pp. 241-244.

Scholl, Richard; Cooper, Elizabeth. 1991. "The use of job evaluation to eliminate gender based pay differentials", in *Public Personnel Management*, Vol. 20, Spring, pp. 1-18.

Schwab, Donald; Grams, Robert. 1985. "Sex related errors in job evaluation: A 'real world' test", in *Journal of Applied Psychology*, Vol. 70, Aug., pp. 533-539.

Schwab, Donald; Wichern, Dean. 1983. "Systematic bias in job evaluation and market wages: Implications for the comparable worth debate", in *Journal of Applied Psychology*, Vol. 68, Feb., pp. 60-69.

Scoville, James; Azevedo, Ross. 1991. "Wage lines and comparable worth: Gainers, losers, and the prospects for free collective bargaining", in *Journal of Collective Negotiations in the Public Sector*, Vol. 20, n.1, pp. 53-67.

Shamie, Stephen. 1986. *Narrowing the gender gap: Is equal value the answer?* (Kingston, Ontario, Queen's University, Industrial Relations Centre).

Shapiro, D.; Stelcner, M. 1987. "The persistence of the male-female earnings gap in Canada, 1978-80", in *Canadian Public Policy*, Dec., pp. 462-476.

Shaw, Bill. 1987. "Comparable worth and its prospects: AFSCME v. State of Washington", in *Labour Law Journal*, Vol. 38, Feb., pp. 100-118.

Shortt, Christine. 1986. "Equal pay - what happened?", in *Journal of Industrial Relations*, Vol. 28, No. 3, pp. 315-335.

Smith, James; Ward, Michael. 1984. *Women's wages and work in the twentieth century* (Santa Monica, California, Rand).

Smith, Robert S. 1988. "Comparable worth: Limited coverage and the exacerbation of inequality", in *Industrial and Labour Relations Review*, Vol. 41, Jan., pp. 227-239.

Sorensen, Elaine. 1984. "Equal pay for comparable worth: A policy for eliminating the undervaluation of women's work", in *Journal of Economic Issues*, Vol. 18, June, pp. 465-472.

–. 1986. "Implementing comparable worth: A survey of recent job evaluation studies", in *American Economic Review*, Vol. 76, May, pp. 364-367.

–. 1987. "Effect of comparable worth policies on earnings", in *Industrial Relations*, Vol. 26, Fall, pp. 227-239.

–. 1989. "The wage effects of occupational sex composition: A review and new findings", in M. A. Hill; M. Killingsworth (eds.), *Comparable worth: Analyses and evidence* (Ithaca, New York, ILR Press).

–. 1990. "The crowding hypothesis and comparable worth", in *Journal of Human Resources*, Vol. 25, pp. 55-89.

SPR Associates Incorporated. 1991. *An evaluation of pay equity in Ontario: The first year* (Toronto, SPR).

Stackpool-Moore, J. 1990. "From equal pay to equal value in Australia: Myth or reality?", in *Comparative Labor Law Journal*, Vol. 11, No. 3, pp. 273-294.

Steinberg, Ronnie. 1986. "The debate over comparable worth", in *New Politics*, Vol. 1, Summer, pp. 108-126.

–. 1990. "Social construction of skill: Gender, power, and comparable worth", in *Work and Occupations*, Vol. 17, Nov., pp. 449-482.

Steinberg, R. et al. 1986. *The New York State Comparable Worth Study: Final Report* (Albany, New York, Center for Women in Government, State University of New York at Albany).

Stonebraker, Peter W.; LaVan, Helen. 1987. "Comparable worth: Issues to resolve before equity can become reality", in *International Journal of Manpower*, Vol. 8, No. 4, pp. 13-19.

Thornton, Margaret. 1981. "(Un)equal pay for work of equal value", in *Journal of Industrial Relations*, Vol. 23, No. 4, pp. 466-481.

–. 1986. "The equality principle and the sexual division of labour", in *Women's Studies International Forum*, Vol. 9, No. 1, pp. 13-18.

Thornton, Robert S. 1986. "The economic case against comparable worth", in *Journal of Collective Negotiations in the Public Sector*, Vol. 15, No. 1, pp. 53-59.

Todres, Elaine. 1987. "With deliberate care: The framing of Bill 154", in *Manitoba Law Journal*, Vol. 16, Spring, pp. 221-226.

Tompkins, Jonathan. 1987. "Comparable worth and job evaluation validity", in *Public Administration Review*, Vol. 47, May-June, pp. 254-258.

Tompkins, Jonathan et al. 1990. "Designing a comparable worth based job evaluation system: Failure of an a priori approach", in *Public Personnel Management*, Vol. 19, Spring, pp. 31-42.

Treiman, Donald J. 1979. *Job evaluation: An analytic review* (Washington, DC, National Academy of Sciences).

Treiman, Donald J.; Hartmann, Heidi (eds.). 1981. *Women, work, and wages: Equal pay for jobs of equal value* (Washington, DC, National Academy of Sciences).

Treiman, Donald J.; Roos, Patricia. 1983. "Sex and earnings in industrial society: A nine-nation comparison", in *American Journal of Sociology*, Vol. 89, Nov., pp. 612-650.

Treu, Tiziano. 1986. "Equal pay and comparable worth: A view from Europe", in *Comparative Labour Law Journal*, Vol. 8, Fall, pp. 1-33.

Turner, David. 1986. "Equal value as a bargaining lever", in *Personnel Management*, June, pp. 38-41.

Tzannatos, Zafiris. 1987. "Equal pay in Greece and Britain", in *Industrial Relations*, Vol. 18, Winter, pp. 275-283.

Tzannatos, P. Z.; Zabaiza, A. 1984. "The anatomy of the rise of British female relative wages in the 1970s: Evidence from the new earnings survey", in *British Journal of Industrial Relations*, Vol. 22, July, pp. 177-194.

US Commission on Civil Rights. 1984. *Comparable worth: Issue for the 80's*, Vols. 1 and 2 (Washington, DC, US Government Printing Office).

–. 1985. *Comparable worth: An analysis and recommendations* (Washington, DC, US Government Printing Office).

US General Accounting Office. 1992. *Pay equity: Washington State's efforts to address comparable worth* (Washington, DC, General Accounting Office).

Volz, William H., and Breitenbeck, Joseph T. 1984. "Comparable worth and the union's duty of fair representation", in *Employee Relations Law Journal*, Vol. 10, Summer, pp. 30-47.

von Prondzynski, Ferdinand. 1988. *Report of the network of experts on the implementation of the equality directives* (Brussels, Commission of the European Community).

Weiler, Paul. 1986. "The wages of sex: The uses and limits of comparable worth", in *Harvard Law Review*, Vol. 99, June, pp. 1728-1807.

–. 1991. "Comparable worth in United States' Antidiscrimination law", in *International Review of Comparative Public Policy*, Vol. 3, pp. 333-352.

Weiner, Nan. 1991. "Job evaluation systems: A critique", in *Human Resources Management Review*, Vol. 1, No. 2, pp. 119-132.

Weiner, Nan; Gunderson, Morley. 1990. *Pay equity: Issues, options and experience* (Toronto, Butterworths).

Werwie, Doris. 1987. *Sex and pay in the federal government: Using job evaluation systems to implement comparable worth* (New York, Greenwood Press).

Wesman, Elizabeth C. 1988. "Unions and comparable worth: Progress in the public sector", in *Journal of Collective Negotiations in the Public Sector* , Vol. 17, No. 1, pp. 13-26.

Willborn, Steven. 1986a. *A comparable worth primer* (Lexington, Massachusetts, Lexington Books).

–. 1986b. "Equal pay for work of equal value: Comparable worth in the United Kingdom", in *American Journal of Comparative Law*, Vol. 34, Summer, pp. 415-457.

–. 1989. *A secretary and a cook: Challenging women's wages in the courts of the United States and Great Britain* (Ithaca, New York, ILR Press).

– (ed.). 1991. *Women's Wages: Stability and change in six industrialized countries*, Vol. 3, *International Review of Comparative Public Policy*.

Zabalza, A.; Tzannatos, Z. 1985a. "The effect of Britain's anti-discriminatory legislation on relative pay and employment", *Economic Journal*, Vol. 95, Sep., pp. 679-699.

–; –. 1985b. *Women and equal pay* (Cambridge, United Kingdom, Cambridge University Press).

DATE DUE